Elena Kagan

by Viqi Wagner

LUCENT BOOKS
A part of Gale, Cengage Learning

GALE
CENGAGE Learning·

Detroit • New York • San Francisco • New Haven, Conn • Waterville, Maine • London

GALE
CENGAGE Learning·

LIBRARY OF CONGRESS CATALOGING-IN-PUBLICATION DATA

Wagner, Viqi, 1953-
  Elena Kagan / by Viqi Wagner.
    p. cm. -- (People in the news)
  Summary: "This series profiles the lives and careers of some of today's most prominent newsmakers. Whether covering contributions and achievements or notorious deeds, books in this series examine why these well-known personages garnered public attention"-- Provided by publisher.
  Includes bibliographical references and index.
  ISBN 978-1-4205-0604-4 (hardback)
  1. Kagan, Elena, 1960- 2. Judges--United States--Biography. 3. United States. Supreme Court--Officials and employees. I. Title.
  KF8745.K34W34 2012
  347.73'2634--dc23
  [B]
                                                2011039642

Lucent Books
27500 Drake Rd.
Farmington Hills, MI 48331

ISBN-13: 978-1-4205-0604-4
ISBN-10: 1-4205-0604-8

Printed in the United States of America
1 2 3 4 5 6 7 16 15 14 13 12

Contents

Fame and celebrity are alluring. People are drawn to those who walk in fame's spotlight, whether they are known for great accomplishments or for notorious deeds. The lives of the famous pique public interest and attract attention, perhaps because their experiences seem in some ways so different from, yet in other ways so similar to, our own.

Newspapers, magazines, and television regularly capitalize on this fascination with celebrity by running profiles of famous people. For example, television programs such as *Entertainment Tonight* devote all their programming to stories about entertainment and entertainers. Magazines such as People fill their pages with stories of the private lives of famous people. Even newspapers, newsmagazines, and television news frequently delve into the lives of well-known personalities. Despite the number of articles and programs, few provide more than a superficial glimpse at their subjects.

Lucent's People in the News series offers young readers a deeper look into the lives of today's newsmakers, the influences that have shaped them, and the impact they have had in their fields of endeavor and on other people's lives. The subjects of the series hail from many disciplines and walks of life. They include authors, musicians, athletes, political leaders, entertainers, entrepreneurs, and others who have made a mark on modern life and who, in many cases, will continue to do so for years to come.

These biographies are more than factual chronicles. Each book emphasizes the contributions, accomplishments, or deeds that have brought fame or notoriety to the individual and shows how that person has influenced modern life. Authors portray their subjects in a realistic, unsentimental light. For example, Bill Gates—cofounder of the software giant Microsoft—has been instrumental in making personal computers the most vital tool of the modern age. Few dispute his business savvy, his perseverance, or his technical expertise, yet critics say he is ruthless in his dealings with competitors and driven more by his desire to maintain Microsoft's dominance in the computer industry than by an interest in furthering technology.

In these books, young readers will encounter inspiring stories about real people who achieved success despite enormous obstacles. Oprah Winfrey—one of the most powerful, most watched, and wealthiest women in television history—spent the first six years of her life in the care of her grandparents while her unwed mother sought work and a better life elsewhere. Her adolescence was colored by pregnancy at age fourteen, rape, and sexual abuse.

Each author documents and supports his or her work with an array of primary and secondary source quotations taken from diaries, letters, speeches, and interviews. All quotes are footnoted to show readers exactly how and where biographers derive their information and provide guidance for further research. The quotations enliven the text by giving readers eyewitness views of the life and accomplishments of each person covered in the People in the News series.

In addition, each book in the series includes photographs, annotated bibliographies, timelines, and comprehensive indexes. For both the casual reader and the student researcher, the People in the News series offers insight into the lives of today's newsmakers—people who shape the way we live, work, and play in the modern age.

Elena Kagan: Bridge Builder on a Divided Supreme Court

On August 7, 2010, Elena Kagan was sworn in as the 112th justice, and fourth woman, to serve on the U.S. Supreme Court. This historic scene had become almost routine in recent years: Four of the nine justices on the highest court in the land have joined the Court since 2005. The buzz of publicity about Elena Kagan, however, was not routine. Amid the usual congratulations from well-wishers and complaints from critics was an unusual amount of curiosity and guesswork.

Three months earlier, when President Barack Obama announced Kagan as his choice to fill the seat of retiring justice John Paul Stevens, the American people and the senators who would have to approve the nomination knew little about the fifty-year-old lawyer. There was no judicial track record of previous decisions on important cases because Kagan had never been a judge. There was not much of a paper trail of her personal views because Kagan keeps her private life and opinions to herself. Kagan also refused to be pinned down during the confirmation process; under questioning, she gave few hints about how she was likely to rule on controversial issues.

A closer look at Kagan's life and career in the law, however, reveals a very smart, likeable, and hardworking woman with a record of groundbreaking achievements. It also reveals what many people see as Kagan's greatest strength: a remarkable ability to get people with strongly held, conflicting views to work together and get things done.

The Supreme Court's Tug-of-War

That is a valuable ability to bring to the current Supreme Court. Just as there is little bipartisanship, or cooperation between Republicans and Democrats, in Congress today, the Supreme Court has a strong conservative wing and a strong liberal wing with not much common ground on divisive issues. There is a political connection between the justices on the Court and the elected officials who put them there: The justices in the conservative, or right, wing are Republican appointees, and the justices in the liberal, or left, wing are Democratic appointees.

The Supreme Court, however, is the third branch of government, not part of the legislative or executive branch. Supreme Court judges are supposed to seek justice impartially, not side with a political party. The labels "conservative" and "liberal" actually refer to the justices' legal views and how they interpret the Constitution, not whether they are Republicans or Democrats.

Conservative judges tend to argue that the courts should not extend constitutional rights or restrictions in new ways. In the conservative way of thinking about government, change should come from Congress and the president, not from judges. Conservatives also think that judges should not strike down laws and presidential decisions that the Constitution gives the legislative and executive branches the right to make, a concept known as judicial restraint.

In contrast, in liberal judges' view the Constitution is a living document that the courts must interpret in light of changing times and the needs of the nation. Liberal judges tend to argue that the courts should not always have to decide a case the way a similar case was decided in the past. In the liberal way of thinking about government, judges should sometimes extend constitutional rights and restrictions in new ways to solve new problems, a concept known as judicial activism.

President Barack Obama, right, with Chief Justice John Roberts, congratulates new Supreme Court justice Kagan after her public investiture ceremony in October 2010.

Such different legal views can lead to split votes and friction on the Court. In nominating Kagan, Obama was betting on her ability to ease friction and help reach consensus on difficult issues. Consensus does not mean unanimous agreement. Consensus means reaching a decision that most people can agree on, using reason, persuasion, and compromise. Consensus decision making aims to bring people on opposite sides closer to the center.

Lifelong Evidence of an Open Mind

Kagan's talent for connecting people—and for connecting *with* people—has been on display since her teenage years. In college she was known for friendships with classmates who held widely differing political views. A feisty liberal herself, as a teacher at the University of Chicago she praised outspoken conservative Supreme Court justice Antonin Scalia for the "quality and intelligence (even if ultimate wrong-headedness)"[1] of his work.

As an aide to Democratic president Bill Clinton, Kagan was known for reaching out to conservative Republicans in Congress and keeping her cool during tough negotiations. As the first female dean of Harvard Law School, she got the famously divided faculty of the famously traditional school to approve new hires, reform the curriculum, and adopt a new grading system. As Obama's solicitor general (the lawyer who represents the U.S. government in cases before the Supreme Court), Kagan seemed to win the respect of Scalia, who enjoyed going toe-to-toe with her in legal arguments.

Kagan's people skills were also tested during her televised Senate confirmation hearings in June and July 2010. Kagan was poised and confident in her appearances before the Senate Judiciary Committee. She lightened the tense atmosphere with humor, and she stayed calm and reasonable when criticized or challenged by her questioners. She came across as someone just as comfortable, energetic, and down-to-earth at the highest levels of government and academia as she is teaching a classroom of first-year law students.

Bipartisan Praise

During the hearings, praise for the Democratic nominee's ability to find common ground and get the job done came from both ends of the political spectrum. One impressive Republican vote of confidence came from Bradford Berenson, former legal counsel in the George W. Bush White House. "Elena is universally well-liked and trusted by lawyers on both the right and the left," Berenson said. "Her congeniality, flexibility, and moderate demeanor would serve her well on the Supreme Court, where she would have uncommon potential to build coalitions and consensus with her colleagues. . . . She could turn out to be a genuinely influential justice."[2]

Another endorsement came in the form of an open letter to the chairmen of the Senate Judiciary Committee signed by sixty-nine deans of American law schools. Kagan had been so effective at Harvard, the deans wrote, "because of her willingness to listen to diverse viewpoints and give them all serious consideration. She revealed a strong and consistent aptitude for forging coalitions that achieved smart and sensible solutions, often in the face of seemingly insoluble conflict."[3]

More bipartisan support came in an open letter from the ten solicitors general who held that job before Kagan, under both Democratic and Republican presidents. They brought up the important point that a Supreme Court justice who had been a solicitor general would have a unique understanding of how legal teams from the Justice Department and the Supreme Court could work together better.

Ready to Go to Work

Supporters and critics alike will be watching and waiting to see if Kagan lives up to her reputation, as cases dealing with same-sex marriage, health-care reform, gun control, abortion, and the detention of terrorist suspects wind their way through the court system. As she began her first term as an associate justice in October 2010, Kagan cheerfully told reporters that she was up to the task, eager to learn from her colleagues, and ready to go to work. In her typical down-to-earth, nonpartisan style, Kagan said simply that she hopes the American people will learn "that I'm an open-minded person, that I'm a fair person, that I have good judgment, that I'll faithfully apply the law and do the best I can to decide it in the right way."[4]

Chapter 1

Coming of Age in a Politically Turbulent Era

Elena Kagan, born into a well-educated, liberal Jewish family in New York City, was raised to take part in the social and political causes of the 1960s and 1970s, such as the antiwar and women's rights movements. Home was the Upper West Side of Manhattan, a traditional center of New York's Jewish community and liberal politics. Much was expected of the bright young men and women of this neighborhood, who dreamed of becoming the leaders of their generation.

Family Origins

Kagan was born in Manhattan on April 28, 1960. Elena (who has no middle name) was the middle child and only daughter of three children born to Robert and Gloria Kagan. Her father was the son of Russian Jewish immigrants who made and sold hats and clothing in Brooklyn. Hardworking and ambitious, Robert Kagan earned a bachelor's degree at Penn State University, a law degree at Yale Law School, and a master's degree in law from New York University.

Elena's mother, Gloria Gittelman Kagan, was also a child of Russian Jewish immigrants. She was raised in Philadelphia, where her parents owned a dairy business. As a girl, Gloria helped her

The Kagans pose for a family photo in 1970, with Elena, age nine, at left, mother Gloria and father Robert, and brothers Irving and Marc.

mother, Esther, behind the store counter while her father, Laizar, delivered eggs, butter, and cheese to markets and diners by truck. Education was an important family value: Gloria graduated from a demanding public school, Philadelphia High School for Girls, and earned a bachelor's degree at Penn State University.

Fellow students at Penn State, Robert and Gloria met by chance on a train during a school holiday. They married in 1950. When Robert finished law school, the couple settled in Stuyvesant Town, a project of red-brick high-rise apartment buildings on Manhattan's East Side.

A Move to the Upper West Side

With partner Bill Lubic, Robert Kagan built a law practice specializing in land-use issues. Kagan made his reputation as a land-use lawyer during an era of great change in New York's housing market. At the time, most ordinary New Yorkers were renters. New rent-control laws that were passed to protect tenants from unfair rent hikes drove a wave of investors and landlords all over New York City to sell off their real estate. Rather than let the old apartment buildings and row houses fall into the hands of developers who might tear down the buildings and evict the residents, tenants banded together to buy their own apartments and run their jointly owned property as a cooperative, or co-op. Kagan was soon in demand by tenant groups who trusted his advice and needed a good lawyer to walk them through the complex co-op conversion process.

One of the co-op conversions the partners handled was the fifteen-story apartment building where the Kagan family moved when Elena was very young: 320 West End Avenue, Apartment 3B, on the Upper West Side of Manhattan. The Kagan family home for more than forty years was a 1,700-square-foot (158 sq. m), two-bedroom co-op with a spacious entryway. It had features typical of New York apartments built before World War II, such as high ceilings and a small maid's room off the kitchen. The book-filled home was comfortable but not luxurious. Elena grew up there with her older brother, Marc, born in 1957, and her younger brother, Irving, born in 1965.

"You Saw a Broad Swath of Life Just Walking Down the Street"

The Upper West Side of Elena's youth was not a fancy place. Gracious, historic high-rises and grand boulevards coexisted with abandoned buildings, run-down storefronts, and gritty Sherman Square, an urban park where heroin was sold openly. The population was a mix of longtime residents, mostly European Jews, and recent arrivals, mostly Puerto Rican, Chinese, and Haitian immigrants. A high school friend says the racial and economic mix was good for Elena: "One of the advantages of growing up in New York in those days was that you saw a broad swath of life just walking down the street. . . . [Elena's] world-view includes a wide range of experience just because of what she saw and where she lived."[5]

Kagan family life in the 1960s and 1970s revolved around school and the Orthodox Lincoln Square Synagogue. The Kagan children were expected to participate in daily dinner-table discussions about their studies and the hot-topic issues of the day: civil rights, women's rights, poverty, the unpopular Vietnam War, the early environmental movement.

Batting around ideas, often noisily, seemed to be a way of life on the Upper West Side. In the late 1960s its residents marched down Broadway holding candles to demonstrate against the Vietnam War. Its newly elected congressional representative was Bella Abzug, a lawyer, social activist, and feminist whose famous campaign slogan was "This woman's place is in the house—the House of Representatives."[6] Elena and her brothers were strongly influenced by their surroundings. They saw first-hand social problems that needed fixing, and they heard new voices telling them they could go anywhere they wanted in life.

Lessons from Parents

Elena and her brothers also absorbed their parents' values: From Robert, the importance of working to make life better for the people of one's community; from Gloria, the importance of bettering oneself.

Social activist and feminist Bella Abzug was elected to Congress in 1970 to represent Manhattan's Upper West Side, the diverse, politically conscious area where Kagan grew up.

Through his work with tenant groups, Robert Kagan became a community leader. He was president of a citywide parents group, the United Parents Association, and in later years a trustee of the West End Synagogue. He was known for battling a huge highway project called Westway, which would have reshaped part of Manhattan through landfill, created more traffic and air pollution, and blocked residents' scenic river views. The defiant Kagan once roped himself to a tree in Riverside Park, determined to stop Westway workers from cutting it down. (Kagan became chair of two neighborhood coalitions that eventually helped defeat Westway.)

Gloria Kagan was a famously tough social studies and language arts teacher at Hunter College Elementary School for twenty years. Elena Kagan describes her mother as the kind of teacher "students remember for the rest of their lives."[7] Mrs.

Kagan's former students agree—though what they remember seems to be a mix of appreciation and childhood terror. "She expected her students to do their homework, to pay attention, to keep their desks clean, to challenge themselves," recalls one of her former fifth-grade students. "And when they didn't, she would express her disappointment. Often you could hear her disappointment through the wall, in Mr. Pantazoni's classroom."[8] Says another, "The words 'iron' and 'fist' come to mind."[9] At least one student took to hiding under her desk in Mrs. Kagan's classroom. Former student Laura Harrington dryly sums up Gloria Kagan's teaching philosophy: "Her value system was to learn something; don't fritter away your time being 12."[10]

Neighbors and friends speak warmly about both Robert and Gloria Kagan, describing the same admirable traits for which Elena would become known. Robert could stay calm in the midst of heated arguments and wrangle agreements from co-op, committee, and synagogue board members. Both parents were proud of Elena's achievements but never boastful.

A Battle Over Bat Mitzvah

Friends say the Kagans were not overbearing with their own children, who were naturally driven and strong willed. As she was about to turn thirteen, for example, Elena clashed with the family's Orthodox rabbi over her bat mitzvah, the coming-of-age ritual for Jewish girls. She wanted a bat mitzvah ceremony equal to the bar mitzvah of Jewish boys—she wanted to lead the service in the synagogue, on a Saturday morning, and read aloud from the Torah.

The rabbi objected. Orthodox Jewish congregations at that time barred girls and women from equal participation in public religious services. In fact, there had never been a formal bat mitzvah at the synagogue. In an early example of her consensus-building talent, Elena and the rabbi worked out a compromise. On May 18, 1973, thirteen-year-old Elena led the first-ever bat mitzvah ceremony at Lincoln Square—but it was a Friday night, and she read from the Book of Ruth.

Varied Paths to Higher Education

Elena's brother Marc, educated at the Dalton School and Yale University, went his own way after college. A social activist, he worked as a forklift mechanic at the 207th Street subway yard and as a union leader before becoming a respected teacher. Her brother Irving earned bachelor's and master's degrees at Yale. Then he, too, followed in his mother's footsteps and became a teacher at Hunter College High School, where Elena went to high school.

Elena was a star student in a high school full of star students. Hunter College High School (which starts in seventh grade) was a top-ranked public school for gifted students from all over New York City and from all racial and ethnic backgrounds. In Elena's time it was an all-girls school. Getting in was based on a tough entrance exam, not money or family connections. Elena's classmate Ellen Purtell recalls, "We were really exposed to tremendous diversity there—whether it was a Jewish girl from the Upper West Side or a cop's kid from the Bronx . . . or kids whose parents worked in sweatshops in Chinatown. It was never about what you were wearing. It was: Did you bring your best game academically with you today and could you contribute to the discussion?"[11]

A sign marks the entrance to the campus of Hunter College High School, where Kagan attended high school.

Hunter graduate Jennifer Raab, today president of the City University of New York's Hunter College, says the school strongly believed in public service: "There was no driver's ed, there was no home economics, you didn't learn to type. You were reading great books and you were going to college. You were going to lead, you were going to give back."[12]

Elena was popular at Hunter. The petite girl with long brown hair and wire-rimmed glasses was funny, fun to be around, and full of energy. She was a serious student and a good listener, more interested in long talks and hanging out in coffee shops than in 1970s fashions or rock music. (Like a lot of native New Yorkers, Elena did not learn to drive a car until her late twenties; one friend says she still does not quite have the hang of it.)

Thinking she might follow her father into the law, Elena played a lawyer in an eighth-grade mock trial. The classmate who played the opposing lawyer remembers being overruled by thirteen-year-old Elena, as confident as a judge, for not following proper legal procedure. At seventeen Elena became president of the student government organization. In a sign of things to come, she posed for the group's yearbook photo in a judge's robe holding a gavel. Beside her senior class photo, she put a quotation by Supreme Court justice Felix Frankfurter: "Government is itself an art, one of the subtlest of arts."[13]

Princeton and Politics

Elena graduated from Hunter in 1977. That fall, she entered elite Princeton University in New Jersey. At this point she thought law was interesting to think about and mattered in people's lives, but becoming a lawyer was just one possibility. With no definite career in mind, she majored in history and explored a range of interests during her four years at Princeton.

On campus Elena became a news writer for the *Daily Princetonian* student newspaper. The paper's staff and faculty sponsors were so impressed by her beautifully written and well-thought-out articles that she was promoted to editorial chair. Up at all hours with a pencil behind her ear, Elena was in charge of overseeing or writing daily unsigned editorials on local and national issues.

The Distinguished Graduates of "the Brick Prison"

New York's Hunter College High School is renowned for academic excellence and for the high percentage of its graduates who go on to top universities. It is also housed in a famously strange building: a four-story, red-brick structure, with fort-like towers at the corners, that takes up an entire city block and has almost no windows. Built to match an old weapons storehouse that once stood there, the school looks like its nickname, "the Brick Prison." Generations of the school's "inmates," as Hunterites call themselves, love to complain about no sunlight and bad air, not to mention mountains of homework.

Elena Kagan was not the only girl in her Hunter class to rise to the top of her profession. The class of 1977 produced lawyers, doctors, distinguished professors, investment bankers, an Associated Press reporter, and even a rocket scientist. Notable Hunterites from other classes include writer Cynthia Ozick, singer Maria Muldaur, actress and civil rights activist Ruby Dee, actress Cynthia Nixon, Tony Award–winning composer-lyricist Robert Lopez, and cardiologist and former American Red Cross president Bernadine Healy. Although Kagan is the first graduate of the Brick Prison to reach the

U.S. Supreme Court, Hunter graduates have served on the state supreme courts of Wisconsin, Pennsylvania, and Connecticut.

Students call the fort-like Hunter College High School "the Brick Prison."

Off campus, in the summer of 1980 she worked fourteen hours a day, six days a week, for the campaign to elect Democrat Liz Holtzman to the U.S. Senate. On election night, when the news came that conservative Republicans had beaten Democrats (including Holtzman) in many congressional races and Republican Ronald Reagan had won the presidency in a landslide, Elena got a little drunk, sat down on the steps at what was supposed to be a victory rally, and cried. Then she wrote an emotional editorial mourning the lack of "real Democrats" in politics—"men and women committed to liberal principles and motivated by the ideal of an affirmative and compassionate government." Elena predicted that Americans would soon turn against the conservatives who had swept into power and that liberalism would come back stronger than ever. For now, though, she wrote, "I wonder how all this could possibly have happened and where on earth I'll be able to get a job next year."[14]

That was perhaps the last time Kagan spoke so openly on record. From then on she never participated in obvious political displays. She did not join political marches or protests. Her coworkers did not know which candidates she supported in her private life or even if she was registered to vote. Her research papers and editorials took a stand based on evidence and reason, but on record she was guarded and never one-sided about her personal views.

She wrote her senior thesis on the Socialist Party and the failure of radical left-wing politics to take hold in America. Elena's term paper, "To the Final Conflict: Socialism in New York City, 1900–1933," would later be a source of controversy in her rise to high government posts.

In 1981 Kagan graduated summa cum laude, with highest honors, from Princeton. The job search she had worried about was postponed when she won a scholarship to continue her studies at Oxford University in England. There she earned a master's degree in philosophy in 1983.

Discovering a Passion for the Law

Shortly after joining the Supreme Court in 2010, Kagan was asked how she became a lawyer in the first place. She admitted

Kagan, third row, sixth from left, poses with the staff of the **Harvard Law Review** *in 1985.*

with a smile that, as dean of a law school, "I used to tell people all the time, 'Don't go to law school just because you don't know what else to do.' But the truth was that's why I went to law school."[15]

At twenty-three, Kagan still had not made up her mind about a career. Back in the United States after two years at Oxford, she figured she would keep her options open, get a law degree, and then decide how to put her education to good use. So Kagan enrolled at Harvard Law School, outside Boston, where she says something unexpected happened: "I was amazed to find that I absolutely *loved* law school."[16] She had always been a good student, but at Harvard Law she finally discovered true passion for a subject.

Kagan made good friends at Harvard, including Jeffrey Toobin, now a legal analyst for CNN and the *New Yorker* magazine. She also snagged one of Harvard Law's most coveted prizes, a spot as an editor on the student-run *Harvard Law Review*. Only second- and third-year students with a combination

Rowing for Oxford

For fun, Elena Kagan joined the women's rowing team during her time at Oxford University. Kagan did not actually pull an oar, however. She was the coxswain, or cox, the pint-sized person with a megaphone who steers the boat from her seat at the rear end. It is hard to imagine a better cox than Kagan. A good cox is small, to keep the boat as light as possible (Kagan is 5 feet 3 inches, or 160cm, tall). A good cox has lung power (growing up in noisy New York was good training). Part cheerleader and part master tactician, the cox studies the course, shouts the orders, and spurs her teammates to row harder and stay in rhythm. A good cox is determined and unflappable, someone who can give and take some boat bumping in tight races. And a good cox has to be a good sport; traditionally, the crew throws the cox in the water after every win.

Kagan had all those qualities. In typical Kagan style, she also enjoyed analyzing and teaching others about the sport. Jason Brown, a friend since Princeton days, says he used to tease her: "How big a deal could it be to yell, 'Stroke! Stroke! Stroke!'" According to Brown, "She explained the intricacies. She insisted it was much more complicated than that."

Quoted in Andrea Stone. "Elena Kagan's Long Journey to High Court Hopeful." *AOL News*, May 10, 2010. www.aolnews.com/2010/05/10/elena-kagans-long-journey-to-high-court-hopeful.

of top grades and top marks on an annual writing competition can become editors of this nationally respected law journal.

In 1986 she earned her Harvard Law degree with high honors. Kagan was well prepared for a brilliant career. Fresh out of Harvard Law School, her stellar academic record would land her two plum jobs that were anything but entry level.

Chapter 2

Climbing the Career Ladder

At twenty-six, Kagan was ready to conquer new worlds. She had earned degrees from three of the world's most prestigious universities. She was determined to make her mark in a career that combined her two passions: law and public service. She also had a key advantage: a network of friends and supporters who would help her succeed. Over the next decade Kagan's abilities and ambition propelled her toward the top of the legal profession.

A Lowly Clerk in High Places

In 1986 Kagan went directly from law school to a job as a law clerk for Judge Abner Mikva of the D.C. Circuit. Law clerks are the foot soldiers of the judicial system. They scour law libraries to research legal opinions for the judge. They write the judge's notes (and sometimes the judge's final opinions) and keep track of the judge's case schedule. They check and recheck citations (references to past cases) for accuracy, and they make sure the formal opinion is in proper form. Most law clerks rotate through a number of one-year or two-year clerkships. Overworked and underpaid, they do not get much sleep. They *do* get real-world experience in how the courts work. They also get a foot in the door on their way to becoming a judge themselves.

Judge Mikva's court, the U.S. Court of Appeals for the D.C. Circuit, is one of thirteen powerful federal appeals courts that cover different geographical sections of the country. These courts are the second-highest level in the court system. Lower-court cases whose verdicts are appealed come before a federal appeals court as the last step before going to the Supreme Court.

Kagan worked for Mikva for a year at a federal courthouse in the heart of Washington, a block from the Capitol. The judge liked and admired his young clerk. "She was a good clerk, one of the best," he recalls. "She told *me* what the law was."[17]

In 1987 Mikva recommended Kagan for a clerkship at the Supreme Court. It was a huge break for the young lawyer. For the 1987–1988 Supreme Court term, Kagan clerked for Justice Thurgood Marshall, one of the most famous judges in the history of the Court and one of Kagan's personal heroes. Recalling the experience, Kagan says she was both thrilled and careful to stay in her place: "You know, I was a 27-year-old pipsqueak and I was working for an 80-year-old giant in the law and a person who, let us be frank, had very strong jurisprudential and legal views. He knew what he thought about most issues. And for better or for worse, he wasn't really interested in [debating] his clerks."[18]

Even if Marshall did not take his clerks under his wing, he noticed Kagan, whom he called "Shorty" and "Little Bits." The spunky Kagan also managed to amuse, if not impress, her fellow clerks by joining in pickup basketball games in the Supreme Court building's top-floor gym, jokingly known since the 1940s as "the highest court in the land."

Discovering a New Passion: Teaching

As the end of the Supreme Court term (and the Ronald Reagan presidency) neared, Kagan decided she really wanted to work for a Democratic administration in Washington. In the summer of 1988 she joined the campaign staff of Democratic presidential candidate Michael Dukakis as a low-level researcher, mostly writing responses to attacks on the Massachusetts governor's record. After Republican George H.W. Bush won the White House in the November election, a disappointed Kagan decided to go into private practice. She passed the bar exam, got her license

Thurgood Marshall

Thurgood Marshall, the grandson of a slave who rose to become the first African American justice on the U.S. Supreme Court, was born in Baltimore in 1908. His railroad-porter father taught him the value of education and the law, and he decided to become a lawyer. But Marshall grew up in a racially segregated America; as a black man he was barred from attending the University of Maryland School of Law.

After earning his law degree at historically black Howard University in Washington, D.C., in 1933, Marshall set out to undo that injustice. He became a civil rights lawyer and chief counsel for the National Association for the Advancement of Colored People (NAACP) in Baltimore. In case after case, he chipped away at laws that separated blacks from whites in education, public places, the armed forces, jobs, and housing. In 1954 he won his most famous case, *Brown v. Board of Education*, in a landmark Supreme Court decision that overturned segregation in public education by ruling that "separate but equal" facilities could never be truly equal.

In 1967 President Lyndon Johnson named Marshall to the Supreme Court. In his twenty-four years as associate justice,

he was a strong supporter of individual rights, especially the rights of criminal suspects, and a strong opponent of the death penalty. Marshall died in 1991 and is buried at Arlington National Cemetery.

Thurgood Marshall was the first African American to serve on the Supreme Court.

to practice law in New York and Washington, D.C., and joined a D.C. law firm.

Two years later, however, Kagan changed direction. She accepted a position as assistant professor of law at the University of Chicago Law School. The job offer came at the urging of

After clerking and a stint in private practice, in 1991 Kagan joined the faculty of the University of Chicago Law School as an assistant professor.

Abner Mikva, her former boss at the D.C. Circuit Court of Appeals. Mikva had left Washington and was now teaching at the law school. He persuaded Kagan that coming to the University of Chicago would be a good career move. He was right, but even better, Kagan turned out to be a natural in the classroom. She loved teaching, and the students in her administrative and constitutional law courses loved her back. She won the law school's best teacher award so often that some colleagues tried to disallow repeat winners.

At Chicago Law, Kagan acquired a reputation for puzzling over tough legal questions with single-minded focus. Fellow professors say she could get so wrapped up in untangling a legal problem that more than once she parked her car on campus and left it running overnight, simply forgetting to turn it off. (They also say she liked to head back to her car after classes, crank up the car radio, and speed off the lot.)

Making Time for Fun

Despite her busy academic workload at Chicago Law, Kagan made time for an active social life. She lived in Lincoln Park, a neighborhood of vintage houses, cathedrals, coffee shops, and bookstores on the north side of Chicago. She visited an aunt who lived in the city, and she liked meeting students for lunch or dinner at a favorite Chicago hangout, Cafe Ba Ba Reeba.

On campus, Kagan was the star of the faculty trivia team, which went head-to-head with student teams in friendly contests. She was also a regular member of the traditional Quadrangle Club, a lively three-times-a-week faculty lunch with only one rule: The diners could only talk about law or politics.

Off campus, lifelong baseball fan Kagan rooted for the White Sox. Colleagues say she dragged them to play-off games, even in freezing weather. She also took up Chicago-style softball, a quirky version of the game played with a huge ball and no gloves.

Kagan's Game: Chicago-Style Softball

Elena Kagan and friends at the University of Chicago were teammates in a game that Chicagoans love as much as deep-dish pizza: Chicago-style softball. This version of traditional softball is played with a supersized ball, 16 inches (40.6cm) around, that starts out hard but gets so squishy after a couple of innings that the game is also known as mush ball. The ball is hard to throw and hard to hit far. It is also hard to catch, because this game is played bare-handed—no gloves, no catcher's gear, no helmets.

The rules of Chicago-style softball are quirky, too. There are ten players on a team instead of nine. Pitchers lob the ball in the usual way, underhand in a high arc, but they are allowed to jump off the mound in any direction before throwing the ball, so batters see balls coming from all angles. Three, not four, balls is a walk. Batters get only two swings—two strikes and you're out, no more foul balls allowed.

Just for fun, a reporter asked Major League Baseball players to take a look at snapshots of the future Supreme Court justice at the plate in a 1993 mush ball game and give her some tips. New York Mets outfielder Jeff Francoeur did not like what he saw: "She's choked way too far up on the bat. . . . Knuckles need alignment. You can tell she's gripping the bat way too hard. . . . And you can't smile at the pitcher or you're gonna get hit. You're gonna get hit." Then the reporter told Francoeur that native New Yorker Kagan was a lifelong Mets fan. "Is she?" Francouer quipped. "Well, tell her I like her then. Tell her she's got a good stance."

Quoted in Mark Newman. "Kagan Knows Importance of Strong Stance." MLB.com, May 11, 2010. http://mlb.mlb.com/news/article.jsp?ymd=20100511&content_id=9967722&vkey=news_mlb&fext=.jsp&c_id=mlb.

The Kagan-Obama Connection

At the University of Chicago, she also met a bright young Illinois state senator who lectured at the law school part-time. Barack Obama, one year younger than Kagan, was a fellow Harvard Law School graduate. Like Kagan, he had liberal ideals but a practical, open-minded way of resolving disagreements. Mikva, a Democrat and a longtime leader in Illinois politics, became an influential ally and booster of both Obama and Kagan.

In 1993 Kagan took a short leave of absence from the University of Chicago to serve as an aide to Senator Joe Biden (then chair of the Senate Judiciary Committee) during the confirmation of Ruth Bader Ginsburg to the Supreme Court. Ginsburg sailed through her Senate committee hearing and was confirmed

President Obama and Kagan, both Harvard Law School graduates with connections to Illinois Democrat Abner Mikva, celebrate her confirmation as Supreme Court justice in August 2010.

by a near-unanimous 96–3 Senate vote. Kagan did not have anything nice to say about the confirmation process, however. She thought it had served no purpose: The senators who questioned Ginsburg at her hearing seemed uninformed and uninterested in her actual legal and political views, which Ginsburg refused to discuss anyway. Kagan later called the process "a vapid and hollow charade."[19]

That year Kagan also kept in close touch with her family in New York. Her mother had retired from teaching. Her father was still an active partner in his law firm until he had heart surgery late in the year. Sadly for the family, his health declined. In July 1994 Robert Kagan died of pneumonia in New York at the age of sixty-seven.

In 1995, after four happy years at the University of Chicago Law School, Kagan was granted tenure, a permanent place on the faculty offered to highly respected scholars. She was tempted to stay, but again fate stepped in, in the person of Abner Mikva. Her mentor had left Chicago and was now chief White House lawyer for President Bill Clinton. Mikva offered Kagan a White House job. Kagan had always wanted to work in a Democratic administration; she jumped at the chance.

Kagan in the White House: "Wicked Smart"

Kagan spent the next four years as a lawyer in the Clinton White House. Her first title was associate White House counsel. In 1997 she got a promotion and a much fancier title: deputy assistant to the president for domestic policy and deputy director of the Domestic Policy Council.

Kagan's job was to advise the president in two ways. First, she worked to make sure his policies and proposed laws were constitutional. Second, she advised him whether bills passed by Congress were constitutional (and could be signed) or unconstitutional (and should be vetoed). Clinton came to rely on Kagan as a walking encyclopedia on any issue that had to do with the Constitution.

She also won fans among the team of Clinton advisers and assistants who worked closely with her. White House chief of staff Erskine Bowles, for example, used to call her the smartest person in the White House. A later chief of staff, John Podesta, agrees: "There are not a lot of slouchers who work there, but even amongst the kind of super achievers that were there, Elena was in a special class. . . . She's wicked smart. She's a first-rate legal intellect." Moreover, says Podesta, Kagan is not the kind of person to blindly follow her boss's orders or tell him only what he wants to hear: "If she thought [the president] was wrong about something . . . she has the personality that would be up in my face . . . or up in Bill Clinton's face if she thought that we were off the law or off what made sense."[20]

Kagan spent a lot of time and energy on antismoking proposals. She had a personal interest in reducing smoking, especially among teenagers: Kagan herself had only recently quit smoking, a habit she picked up in her teens. (In high school she and fellow smokers had even persuaded the principal to set aside one bathroom where the girls were allowed to take cigarette breaks.) Though she confesses she still enjoys an occasional cigar, Kagan was eager to strengthen the government's antismoking policies.

Clinton made Kagan lead negotiator on a bill that would give the U.S. Food and Drug Administration the authority to regulate Big Tobacco, the nation's major cigarette manufacturers. She was assigned to wrestle over the wording of the bill with the lawmaker who would sponsor it in Congress, Republican senator John McCain. Though that bill did not pass, Kagan won the respect of McCain and other Republicans in the Senate, including physician Bill Frist.

Working on the tobacco bill brought out another Kagan talent: helping Clinton's speechwriters translate technical language into clear messages the American people could understand. She worked on tobacco speeches with Josh Gottheimer, who says she could "take some of the toughest issues and sometimes very complicated issues and put them into plain speak, which as a speechwriter is, of course, a really appreciated and easily digestible way of looking at things. It helps us a lot."[21]

She also worked closely with Neera Tanden, an aide to First Lady Hillary Clinton, on a big proposal to invest $20 billion in child-care programs such as Head Start, after-school learning programs, and the child-care tax credit. Tanden, too, has high praise for Kagan:

> I learned from Elena a great deal about how to develop and work on policy in two key areas. First of all, Elena is a great mentor, but [she] also taught us how to ask the tough questions to really round out how to make smart policy. And also she was very much animated by how policy actually affected real people, real families and the struggle that families have in balancing [work and] family.[22]

In May of 1998 Kagan, left, in background, was a Supreme Court judicial clerk assigned to work on the wording of the Big Tobacco regulation bill with Senator John McCain (seated, left) and other Republican senators.

A Few Stumbles

Kagan's toughness did rub some people the wrong way. What some saw as focus and a can-do attitude, others saw as a demanding, bulldozing style. Her assertiveness might have been a mark against her in 1999, when Clinton nominated Kagan for a judgeship on the D.C. Circuit, the same appeals court where she had clerked for Mikva. Clinton had enemies of his own in the Republican-controlled Congress. His opponents let the nomination sit without a vote until Clinton left office, and that was that. Clinton's Republican successor, George W. Bush, would name another up-and-coming lawyer, John G. Roberts Jr., to the open spot on the D.C. Circuit. Only six years later, Roberts would become Chief Justice of the Supreme Court.

During her decade at Chicago Law and the White House, Kagan published fewer articles than some expected from an expert on constitutional law. Her published writing was mostly book reviews and a few scholarly papers in law journals about First Amendment issues, such as the government's right to regulate pornography and hate speech. One Kagan article, however, would later get plenty of publicity. It was a 1995 review of *The Confirmation Mess*, a book by Stephen Carter. Carter's book is a history of the face-offs between presidential nominees to the Supreme Court and the senators who have to approve or reject the nominees.

In her article Kagan criticizes senators for not asking, and nominees for not answering, probing questions about the nominee's views on controversial issues such as "privacy rights, free speech, race and gender discrimination, and so forth."[23] Kagan says senators have the right and the duty to ask a nominee about "the votes she would cast, the perspective she would add . . . , and the direction in which she would move the [Court],"[24] on such subjects as the death penalty and gun control. Nominees likewise have a duty to give honest answers and defend their views in a real debate. Otherwise, she argues, hearings are just a waste of time. The only thing a nominee should not do, Kagan writes, is express a "settled intent"[25] to vote a certain way; that is, she should not declare that her mind is already made up on a particular case. The arguments Kagan made in this 1995 article would get her in hot water years later, at her own Senate confirmation hearings, when *she* was the person facing probing questions she did not want to answer.

Unable to Go Back, Kagan Goes Forward

As the two-term Clinton presidency came to an end, White House staffers had to figure out what to do next. When it looked like the judgeship was going to fall through, Kagan decided she wanted to go back to teaching at the University of Chicago Law School. In 1999 she applied to rejoin the faculty and resume her old job. To her surprise, the answer was no. Some members of the hiring committee voted to welcome her back, but most felt that her heart really was not set on teaching there. They wanted a long-term commitment; they did not want Kagan to think of Chicago as a good but temporary job while she waited for a better offer from Washington.

So Kagan was out of a job—but not for long. She had a reputation as a first-rate legal thinker and an excellent teacher. She had proved herself as a very competent lawyer in private practice and in the federal government. Soon she would get her chance to excel in a third setting, her alma mater Harvard Law School.

Chapter 3

From the White House to Academia and Back

Elena Kagan left the Bill Clinton White House with her future wide open. She was thirty-nine, single, and free to look anywhere for her next job. In the next decade she would land not one but two of the most prestigious positions in the legal profession: dean of Harvard Law School and U.S. solicitor general. Both jobs demanded sharp skills and the ability to juggle many roles: teacher, scholar, lawyer, administrator, problem solver, and trailblazer.

Return to Harvard

Rejected by Chicago Law but still eager to get back into teaching, in 1999 Kagan applied and was hired as a visiting professor on the faculty at Harvard Law School. She had been a star student there herself thirteen years earlier. Now she had firsthand experience working for a president and applying the Constitution at the highest level of government. Back in academia, she put her new expertise to use in front of the classroom. She taught classes on constitutional law and a seminar on the presidency as well as courses on administrative law and civil procedure.

At Harvard Law, just as at Chicago Law, Kagan was popular and well respected. She had some of her mother's strictness,

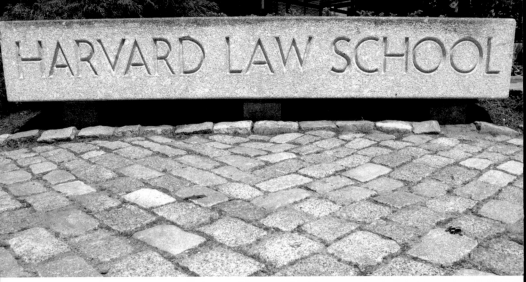

A sign designates the entrance to the campus of Harvard Law School, where Kagan joined the faculty as a visiting professor in 1999.

though. According to one Boston reporter, "She was . . . a clear and enthusiastic teacher, but an unforgiving one as well, known for angrily dressing down students who came to class unprepared."[26]

Kagan wrote one article at this time that got a lot of attention (and would get even more attention when she was nominated for the Supreme Court). Published in 2001, "Presidential Administration" was named one of the year's top scholarly articles by the American Bar Association. In it she discussed three recent presidents who set out to give themselves more control over federal agencies. Kagan was generally in favor of giving the president more power (within limits), even if presidents use this power in opposite ways: Two of the presidents she profiled used it to decrease government oversight, and one used it to increase government oversight.

Dean Kagan

Two years after arriving at Harvard, Kagan was granted tenure and the title of full professor. That honor was eclipsed by a much greater honor two years later, when the dean of the law school, Robert C. Clark, stepped down after fourteen years as head of the school. In April 2003 Elena Kagan was named the new dean of Harvard Law School. She was the first female dean, and only the eleventh dean altogether, in the famed school's 186-year history.

Nearly all of the men who held the title of dean before Kagan had also accepted the honorary title of Sir Isaac Royall Professor of Law. Showing her commitment to civil rights and racial equality, Dean Kagan broke with this tradition. Instead of assuming a professorship named for Royall, a slaveholder in colonial America, she asked to be named Charles Hamilton Houston Professor of Law, in honor of a distinguished African American graduate of Harvard Law School who spent his career fighting segregation.

A Mom's Reaction

Gloria Kagan, who died in 2008, did not live to see her daughter, Elena, become a Supreme Court justice or U.S. solicitor general. She did, however, see Elena become the first female dean of Harvard Law School in 2003. Francine Russo, the Kagans' longtime neighbor in New York, thinks it was Gloria who anonymously posted a *New York Times* clipping about Elena's achievement by the tenants' mailboxes in the lobby of their apartment building. But Mrs. Kagan was never one to brag about her children. When Russo ran into her on the day of the announcement, she says Gloria's reaction to the news of this groundbreaking honor was a shrug. Then, Russo says, "she nodded, unsmiling, and sighed in that stoic way that was now so familiar to me. 'Yeah . . .' then a long silence . . . 'but I really wish she were married.'"

Francine Russo. "What Elena Kagan's Mother Would Really Have Said." *Huffington Post*, May 10, 2010. www.huffingtonpost.com/francine-russo/what-elena-kagans-mother_b_570540.html.

Robert C. Clark, left, outgoing dean of Harvard Law School, and university president Lawrence Summers announce Kagan as the school's new dean in April 2003.

When she took over as dean, tradition-bound Harvard Law School had some big problems. Parts of the curriculum, which focused on training lawyers for the business world, had not been updated in over one hundred years. The aging faculty was divided into feuding camps that bickered over new hires. Students were unhappy, stuck in big classes with distant professors and not much racial diversity. Year after year, the school suffered a blow to its pride when *U.S. News & World Report* ranked Harvard Law below its number one rival, Yale.

Fresh Ideas

Willing to experiment, Kagan set out to transform the school's curriculum, faculty, student life, and budget. Before long she established herself as a very popular leader among students and faculty alike.

Kagan persuaded the faculty to unanimously approve a modernized first-year curriculum. She replaced out-of-date courses with new courses on environmental law, international law, and public law. She added more legal clinics, led by attorneys, to help students understand the connection between legal studies and legal practice. Kagan's most civic-minded new idea: The third year of Harvard Law School is free for all students who agree to work at least five years in public service after they graduate.

Kagan says she learned from Clinton that small changes could help solve big problems. She applied that lesson as dean. As she said in a 2008 interview, "When I got here I looked around for little things I could do: things that don't cost much money, don't take much time, that you don't have to have a faculty meeting to do."[27] Thanks to Kagan, Harvard Law students got free coffee and bagels. The student center got a facelift and better gym equipment. Outside on the lawn she put a beach volleyball court that could be turned into a skating rink in the winter. These small improvements had a big effect on student morale.

Kagan also put her people skills to work in a major fundraising campaign. By 2008 Harvard Law's Setting the Standard campaign had raised over $476 million, the most successful effort in legal education history. (Kagan shared in this success; her annual salary during her years as dean rose to approximately $437,000.)

Fresh Talent

Kagan used some of Harvard Law's new funds to go shopping for talented new faculty members. She went after star professors at rival universities and experts in new fields such as cyberspace law. Her hiring spree added more than forty permanent faculty members, allowed her to shrink class size, boosted the school's image, and led the school newspaper to run the April Fool's Day headline "Dean Kagan Hires Every Law Professor in the Country."[28]

Saying it was healthy for everyone to be exposed to a wide range of opinion, she brought in people with a mix of political viewpoints and backgrounds. For example, she hired Jack Goldsmith, a Justice Department official under President George W. Bush, over the objections of some professors who accused Goldsmith (incorrectly) of writing memos justifying the use of torture. Despite grumbling from liberal-leaning professors, she also hosted a dinner in honor of outspoken conservative Supreme Court justice Antonin Scalia. Says Harvard Law professor Charles Fried, "I think she knocked a few heads, but she worked by and large by persuasion. . . . She got most people on board, and other people fell in line."[29]

Students walk past Harvard Law School's Langdell Hall. During her tenure as dean, Kagan oversaw broad changes to the school's curriculum as well as small changes to improve student life.

Kagan's changes added up to one big basic change at Harvard Law. According to the head of the school's admissions committee, "Before, every possible change had to be weighed against hundreds of years of illustrious history. Now changes are weighed by asking whether it might make something better."[30]

The Don't Ask, Don't Tell Controversy

Kagan was involved in one ongoing controversy during her years as Harvard dean. Harvard had an antidiscrimination policy that required employers, including the military, who wanted to recruit through the school's career office to sign a statement that they do not discriminate on the basis of race, religion, or sexual orientation. Under the policy known as Don't Ask, Don't Tell, however, openly gay men and women were not allowed to serve in the U.S. armed forces. Military recruiters were therefore banned from Harvard.

In 1996 Congress passed a law, called the Solomon Amendment, that blocked federal funding to any school that banned military recruiting on campus. In 2002, standing to lose $328 million in federal grants, Harvard Law lifted its ban on military recruiting while it challenged the Solomon Amendment in court.

As dean, Kagan made sure military recruiters had access to students according to the terms of the Solomon Amendment, but she wrote a letter to the student body condemning Don't Ask, Don't Tell. It read in part, "I believe the military's discriminatory employment policy is deeply wrong—both unwise and unjust. This wrong tears at the fabric of our own community by denying an opportunity to some of our students that other of our students have."[31]

Answering a New President's Call

In 2006 Harvard University president Lawrence Summers resigned after a short, unpopular term in that prestigious position. Kagan was seen as a front-runner to replace Summers. She did not get the job. Glad she was still their dean, more than six hundred Harvard Law students threw a party for her anyway, wearing T-shirts that read "I ♥ Elena."[32]

But three years later, Washington again came calling. Shortly after being elected the first African American president, Barack Obama asked her to be his first solicitor general (SG), one of the highest posts in the Justice Department. It was another ground-breaking opportunity. If approved by the Senate, Kagan would be the first female SG in U.S. history.

"The Tenth Justice"

When Elena Kagan was sworn in as U.S. solicitor general (SG) on March 20, 2009, she took on what has been called "the most important job you've never heard of." The SG has a bigger say in shaping U.S. legal policy than anyone except the president and the attorney general. First, when the federal government has a stake in a case before the Supreme Court, the SG stands before the justices and argues on behalf of the government. Doing that thirty or forty times a year makes the SG staff the most familiar lawyers in the courtroom—the SG even has a second office in the Supreme Court building. Second, the justices actually rely on the SG to carry out their own duties: Even when the government is *not* involved in a case, the Court asks the SG for an opinion on hundreds of pending appeals, including whether to hear or deny these petitions. More than 80 percent of the time, the justices follow the SG's recommendation.

The SG is powerful in a third way. Every year, the government loses hundreds of cases in lower courts. The SG is the person who decides whether or not to appeal those verdicts to a higher court. Just as the Supreme Court justices choose which appeals they want to hear, the SG chooses which government cases to send to the Supreme Court. For all these reasons, the solicitor general is traditionally known as "the tenth justice."

Alexander Wohl. "Bush's Tenth Justice." *American Prospect,* April 25, 2001. http://prospect .org/cs/articles?article=bushs_tenth_justice.

Kagan later joked about the job title, "Nobody knows quite what that means. Some people think it's the people who put the labels on the cigarette packages, but . . . that's the surgeon general."[33] The solicitor general is the person who officially represents the United States—that is, the federal government—in cases that come before the Supreme Court. It is a very busy job; in one way or another, the Solicitor General's Office participates in about two-thirds of Supreme Court cases.

Kagan wanted the job and was willing to take a big pay cut for it. (The SG is paid an annual salary of $165,300.) Money had never been the main draw for Kagan. She was attracted to jobs that involve solving challenging problems and using law to make the world work better. She was also ambitious. Though she did not come right out and say her ultimate goal was a seat on the Supreme Court, she knew the job would be a great stepping-stone to the bench, especially for a lawyer who had not yet been a judge and not yet argued a case before the high court.

The Nominee Faces the Senate

In January 2009 Kagan left Harvard Law a much stronger place than she had found it six years earlier. Like all appointees to high federal office, she prepared to go before a Senate committee for questioning before the Senate voted to approve or reject her nomination.

She was relaxed and confident at her February 10 confirmation hearing. In her opening statement she paid tribute to Thurgood Marshall, for whom she had had the good fortune of clerking at the Supreme Court twenty-two years earlier:

> Justice Marshall had some awfully good jobs in his life. But he always said that the best, bar none, was being Solicitor General. . . . I think he must have been so deeply moved to walk into the most important court in this country when it was deciding its most important cases and to say, "I represent the United States of America." And I think he would have liked that a former clerk of his would be nominated for the same job.[34]

At one point Senator Tom Coburn (R-OK) noted Kagan's lack of courtroom experience and asked her how she would prepare to argue a case before the Supreme Court. She replied with a little New York boldness that when you stand at that podium the important thing is not how many times you have been there before, but what you bring up there with you: "I bring up a lifetime of learning and study of the law, and particularly of the constitutional and administrative law issues that form the core of the Court's docket. I think I bring up some of the communication skills that have made me—I'm just going to say it—a famously excellent teacher."[35]

Kagan was careful, however, not to come across as *too* confident. "I like to think that one of the good things about me is that I know what I don't know," she told the Senate panel, "and that I figure out how to learn it when I need to learn it."[36]

The most uncomfortable part of the hearing for Kagan was being asked to explain why she would not go into detail about her specific views on legal issues. After all, she had once written that nominees *should* be pressed to give frank, revealing answers to senators' tough questions. Kagan still felt honest, open discussion was the ideal way to conduct a confirmation hearing. In the fourteen years since writing her article, however, she had come to believe that a lot of politicians were unable to separate the goals of their party from their duty to evaluate a nominee fairly. She felt too many senators asked for a nominee's opinion on a controversial issue only to find out if it agreed with their party line. If it didn't, they voted no, regardless of the nominee's qualifications for the job.

So, like most other nominees, Kagan dodged specific questions. She told the Senate panel that she and her ideas had matured since 1995: "I wrote that when I was in the position of sitting where the staff is now and feeling a little bit frustrated that I really wasn't understanding completely what the judicial nominee in front of me meant and what she thought."[37]

Kagan passed the test. She was confirmed by the full Senate by a vote of 61–31 and sworn in a day later, on March 20, 2009. She had broken another glass ceiling and become the first female U.S. solicitor general.

Kagan testifies before the Senate Judiciary Committee in February 2009 during hearings to confirm her nomination by President Obama to the post of solicitor general.

The Solicitor General Faces the Supreme Court

The Solicitor General's Office has a staff of about twenty attorneys. The SG argues only the most significant cases in person. Kagan's first appearance before the Court was significant indeed. In September 2009 she argued the case of *Citizens United v. Federal Election Commission*.

The government's position in *Citizens United* was that free speech by corporations and unions—namely, how much they spend on political advertising—is not the same thing as free speech by individuals. Therefore, she argued, corporate political speech can be banned or censored. The government argued that if corporations can spend as much as they like on election ads and do not have to report where that money came from, then rich special interest groups (and even foreign governments) could flood the media with political messages, drown out candidates they oppose, and swing elections. The other side argued that the corporate owners of newspapers such as the *Washington Post* were already allowed to publish unlimited political opinions, so any other corporation should have the same freedom of speech.

Kagan's debut did not go well. During her thirty-minute oral argument to the Court, Chief Justice John Roberts shot thirty questions at her, mostly critical. The government lost the case 5–4.

Kagan personally argued five more cases, on such issues as the placement of a cross on government land and what kinds of support can legally be given to groups listed as terrorist organizations. Some of her oral arguments drew more testy questions from the chief justice, who seemed to want to make her squirm. This led to speculation about a rivalry and rumors that Kagan

An artist's rendering shows Solicitor General Kagan arguing the case of Citizens United v. Federal Election Commission before the Supreme Court in September 2009.

and Roberts just do not like each other. Most people dismissed the rumors, saying tense debate is normal between the justices and the lawyers who face them; that is why it is called arguing a case.

Now and then, Kagan managed to loosen the tense atmosphere in the courtroom. She once took her turn at the podium following a tall lawyer from the other side. As she hand-cranked the podium and its attached microphone down to her level, she made light of their height difference, joking to the justices a few feet away, "This could take a while."[38]

Passed Over, but Not for Long

In 2009, not long after Kagan arrived at the Solicitor General's Office, Obama considered and interviewed her for a possible nomination to the Supreme Court seat vacated by Justice David Souter, who had just announced his retirement. Ultimately, the president nominated Sonia Sotomayor, who took her seat as the new Supreme Court justice in August. Within a year, however, it would be Kagan's turn.

Chapter 4

Reaching the Pinnacle: The Supreme Court Confirmation Process

O n April 9, 2010, John Paul Stevens, soon to turn ninety, announced his retirement after thirty-four years on the Supreme Court of the United States—SCOTUS for short. Stevens was the bow tie–wearing leader of the Court's liberal wing. He was an opponent of the death penalty and a defender of abortion rights, gay rights, and judges' right to interpret the laws and curb presidential power. It was assumed that Barack Obama would nominate a liberal to replace him, so the balance of the Court was not expected to change dramatically. Nonetheless, there were several likely candidates for the job. SCOTUS watchers placed their bets and waited for the president to announce his choice.

On May 10 Obama chose Elena Kagan. He officially tapped his fifty-year-old solicitor general (SG) in a speech at the White House, with a beaming Kagan at his side and her brothers in the audience. Obama called her a brilliant legal mind, someone who welcomed different points of view and shared his own belief in consensus building.

Obama's second nomination equaled the most appointments for any first-term president. Kagan and Sonia Sotomayor could be Obama's longest-lasting legacy, because SCOTUS justices are appointed for life. Everyone thinking about Kagan's fitness for the job had to keep in mind that she might serve for decades. Soon it seemed that everyone *was* thinking about, and shouting about, Kagan's fitness for the job.

Anti-Kagan Claims

In the media circus that followed Obama's announcement, the biggest complaint about Kagan was that she lacked experience. Critics argued that because she had never been a judge, there was no way to grade her judicial skills or know where she stands on important legal issues. Besides, every justice appointed since 1972 had been a judge: Some critics claimed that judicial experience has become a SCOTUS requirement. Not knowing where to put Kagan on the political map, opponents attacked her from all sides.

Kagan looks on as President Obama formally presents her as his choice to replace the retiring Justice John Paul Stevens on the Supreme Court.

Liberals (mostly Democrats) said she was too conservative. As Kagan's 2001 article about presidents who took more control over federal agencies showed, there was common ground between Kagan and conservatives who believe in strong presidential powers. Liberals also blamed Kagan for caving in to military recruitment at Harvard instead of standing by the school's antidiscrimination policy. She came under fire for agreeing with George W. Bush officials that the fight against terrorism was legally a war and that terrorist suspects, like soldiers captured in a battle, did not have the same legal rights as other criminal suspects. Liberal columnist Glenn Greenwald wrote that there were just too many "disturbing risks" and "serious red flags"[39] about Kagan to put her on the high court.

Conservatives (mostly Republicans) said she was too liberal. Opposing the Solomon Amendment at Harvard was called evidence that she was antimilitary. Her college paper on socialism was called evidence that she was a socialist and a radical, labels often pasted on Obama, too. Conservative activist Phyllis Schlafly called Kagan "Obama in a skirt."[40] An editorial in the right-wing *Washington Times* called her corrupt and incompetent, "a radical leftist who would rubber-stamp Mr. Obama's . . . socialist agenda."[41]

There was plenty of anti-Kagan feeling on personal grounds, too. There were rumors that the never-married, childless Kagan is gay; claims that, likewise, she would not understand family issues; claims that she gets too emotionally involved in issues she cares about to be fair. Finally, there was anti-Kagan feeling that had nothing to do with Kagan: In the polarized Congress, most Republican senators were going to vote against anyone nominated by the Democratic president.

Pro-Kagan Claims

The White House countered Kagan critics with a steady stream of press releases packed with quotes from high-ranking officials in support of the SG. Kagan supporters said it should not matter that she had never been a judge. In fact, 40 of the 111 Supreme Court justices before Kagan had never been a judge.

The Supreme Court Confirmation Process in U.S. History

Elena Kagan's confirmation to the U.S. Supreme Court was a process that has been repeated 160 times in U.S. history. Its source is the Constitution, which gives the president the right to name judges to the Supreme Court, but only "by and with the advice and consent" of the Senate. Today this process is long and often disputed, but it did not start out that way. In 1789, when the high court was formed, President George Washington simply submitted a nominee's name in a letter carried to the Senate chamber. By a voice vote taken on the same day, the full Senate gave its approval. Then the nominee was promptly sworn in and took his place on the Court.

Of the 112 justices successfully appointed to the bench, 4 have been women. Two have been African American. One is of Hispanic descent. Historically, most justices have been Protestant, but there are no Protestants on the current Court. There have been thirteen Catholic and eight Jewish justices. The longest-serving justice was William O. Douglas, who spent 36 years and 209 days on the bench. There is no minimum or maximum age for serving on the Supreme Court: The youngest appointee was Joseph Story, thirty-two years old when he was confirmed in 1812. The oldest justice in U.S. history was Oliver Wendell Holmes Jr., who retired at ninety in 1932.

U.S. Constitution, Article 2, Section 2.

(Before 1851, no Supreme Court justice had even earned a law degree.) Tom Goldstein of *SCOTUSblog* wrote that Kagan's work for two presidents had given her valuable, practical governing experience, and that her varied career was better than one spent entirely in the courtroom ("the judicial monastery") or the university ("the ivory tower"[42]). Besides, no paper trail meant there was less chance senators from either party could twist her words in unfair attacks.

The pro-Kagan side cried foul when she was accused of siding with Bush policies in the war on terror. When Kagan talked about giving the president more power, supporters said, she meant power to regulate business and independent federal agencies, not the kinds of power Bush was accused of abusing, such as ordering illegal surveillance and torture.

Many supporters thought Kagan would be a good sparring partner for the outspoken Supreme Court justice Antonin Scalia. Like Kagan, Scalia was known for his intelligence, quick wit, and writing skills. With a reputation as one of the country's finest legal scholars, Kagan could hold her own against more conservative justices. Perhaps she could persuade justices who were wavering on a case to agree with her position. Scalia himself threw Kagan a little support: "Currently, there is nobody on the Court who has *not* served as a judge. . . . I am happy to see that this latest nominee is not a federal judge—and not a judge at all."[43]

As for claims that since college Kagan had been a radical with socialist or communist sympathies, her Princeton professor and thesis adviser, historian Sean Wilentz, came to her defense: "Studying something doesn't necessarily mean that you endorse it. It means you're into it. That's what historians do." Wilentz, who calls Kagan "very vital, very vivacious" and "one of the most extraordinary people I've met in my life," tried to put this issue to rest:

> Elena Kagan is about the furthest thing from a socialist. Period. And always had been. Period. . . . She's a woman whose deepest dedication is to the constitution of the United States. Which some people can think is a terribly radical [extreme left-wing] thing, and some people can think is a terribly reactionary [extreme right-wing] thing, but I think is exactly where she ought to be for the position she is being considered for.[44]

Friends and associates, both male and female, came forward to squelch the rumors that Kagan is a lesbian. Several stated publicly that Kagan is not gay; dated men in law school, in Washington, and in Chicago; and just did not find the right person. Kagan appears to be a contented single woman who is quite satisfied with her life. She rolls her eyes about her mother's wish that she were married and will say no more on the subject.

Prior to her nomination to the Court, Kagan had expressed her views on several hot-button issues, including gay marriage, the death penalty, and gun control.

Kagan on the Record

Amid the media circus, Kagan's past writings did offer some sense of her views on wedge issues; that is, the issues Americans are deeply divided on. They reflect a fine mind reluctant to view the world as black and white or the Constitution as absolute. Her Harvard letter, for example, showed her support for lifting the ban on gays in the military. During her 2009 confirmation for solicitor general, however, she wrote, "There is no federal constitutional right to same-sex marriage."[45]

Kagan has stated that the death penalty is constitutional. In her view, so is the detention of terrorist suspects indefinitely, without trial. She has written that the Constitution protects a woman's right to abortion but gives the states some oversight. On the issue of gun control, Kagan views the right to bear arms like any other constitutional right—fundamental, within limits. (The best-known example of this idea is that the right to free speech does not mean someone can shout "Fire!" in a crowded theater.)

As for the proper role of judges, Kagan supports judicial restraint up to a point. She thinks Congress and the president should have broad powers, without interference from activist judges, as long as they cooperate and the results are forward-moving, or progressive. As she wrote in 2009, "I think it is a great deal better for the elected branches to take the lead in creating a more just society than for the courts to do so."[46]

The Senate Hearings Begin

On June 28 all eyes turned to the Hart Senate Office Building in Washington for Kagan's televised Senate confirmation hearings. For the next four days, the Senate Judiciary Committee grilled Kagan and heard testimony from witnesses on both sides of the appointment.

Kagan's opening statement began with formalities. She thanked the president for nominating her. She thanked the more than eighty senators who had met with her privately in recent weeks. (These traditional courtesy visits are polite and

Kagan appears before the Senate Judiciary Committee to begin confirmation hearings on her nomination to the Supreme Court in June 2010.

brief. Senators who want to put the nominee on the spot save their barbs and speeches for when the television cameras are running.)

Then Kagan's remarks turned personal as she thanked her late parents. She praised Robert and Gloria Kagan as role models of determination, public service, and commitment to learning: "My parents lived the American dream. They grew up in immigrant communities; my mother didn't speak a word of English until she went to school. But she became a legendary teacher and my father a valued lawyer. And they taught me and my two brothers . . . that this is the greatest of all countries, because of the freedoms and opportunities it offers its people."[47]

Kagan told the committee that she had learned equally valuable lessons at Harvard and in government service: respect for the democratic process, the importance of listening to opposing viewpoints with an open mind, and, quoting Justice Stevens, the habit of "understanding before disagreeing."[48]

Her conclusion was quiet and dignified: "I will make no pledges this week other than this one—that if confirmed, I will remember and abide by these lessons. I will listen hard, to every party before the Court and to each of my colleagues. I will work hard. And I will do my best to consider every case impartially, modestly, with commitment to principle, and in accordance with law."[49]

The Senators Ask, the Nominee (Sort of) Answers

Kagan is certainly smart enough and mature enough to have strong opinions of her own. All she would tell the Senate panel, though, is that there was no point in discussing her passions because they would not have any effect on her decisions. Again and again, senators reminded her that she once said nominees should have to explain their political views. Again and again, Kagan insisted that "my politics would be, must be, have to be

Kagan gestures while answering a question during her Senate confirmation hearings in June 2010. She often used humor to break the tension during the otherwise intense questioning by the Senate panel.

Hon. Elena Kagan

completely separate from my judging. Judging is about considering how the law applies to the case, not how your own personal views might suggest anything about the case."[50] She also refused to criticize any Supreme Court decisions of the past sixty years.

She took a middle-of-the-road stance on questions about how she would interpret the Constitution. She agreed with the conservative view that the Constitution is immutable, meaning it cannot be changed except by amendment. Nevertheless, Kagan argued, society *is not* immutable, and the Constitution is not a straitjacket. Courts constantly have to apply the Constitution to new situations. Judges cannot always rely on prior rulings to make wise decisions.

On the second day a little Kagan humor helped break up the tension. Senator Arlen Specter (D-PA) asked her what would be the impact of televising Supreme Court oral arguments. (SCOTUS has never allowed cameras in the courtroom. At the time, Specter was trying to pass a bill to require live broadcasts, but only one justice, Sotomayor, liked the idea.) Said Kagan, "It means I'd have to get my hair done more often, Senator."[51]

Kagan's quick wit won applause when Senator Lindsey Graham (R-SC) asked her where she was on the Christmas Day 2009 attempted airplane bombing, in which Umar Farouk Abdulmutallab tried to blow up a flight to Detroit with explosives hidden in his underwear. Kagan thought he was asking where she stood legally on the issue of arresting the bomber. "No," Graham drawled, "I was just asking where you were on Christmas." Laughing, Kagan made the sly point that there was not much open for non-Christians on Christmas Day: "You know," she quipped, "like all Jews, I was probably at a Chinese restaurant."[52]

She refused to stoop to dumb jokes, though. On the third day of questioning, Senator Amy Klobuchar (D-MN) tried to get Kagan to rule on which hero should win the heroine in the blockbuster *Twilight* movies: "I keep wanting to ask you about the famous case of Edward versus Jacob or the vampire versus the werewolf."[53] With a tight smile, Kagan replied, "I wish you wouldn't,"[54] and waited for the next question.

Justice Kagan

As it turned out, the Senate hearings were not a bruising ordeal. There were no fireworks at the hearings themselves. The Senate investigation uncovered no scandal and no embarrassing incidents in Kagan's past. After seventeen hours of testimony, Kagan was excused, and the show, for now, was over.

On July 20 the Senate Judiciary Committee voted 13–6 to recommend that Kagan be confirmed by the full Senate. On August 5 the full Senate did just that by a vote of 63–37. As in the Judiciary Committee, the vote was mostly along party lines. All but one Democrat voted yes; all but five Republicans voted no.

Two days later Kagan was sworn in by Chief Justice John Roberts in a Saturday ceremony at the Supreme Court. First, in a private room with only her family present, Kagan took the same federal oath of office repeated by members of Congress: "I do solemnly swear that I will support and defend the Constitution of the United States against all enemies, foreign and domestic;

Kagan is sworn in as a member of the Supreme Court by Chief Justice John Roberts, right, in August 2010. Jeffrey Minear, counselor to the chief justice, holds the Bible during the oath.

Antonin Scalia

The justice to whom Elena Kagan is most often compared is Antonin Scalia. The two are opposites in many ways and often on opposite sides of a case, but they have a similar ability to make sparks fly in legal debate. Scalia, known as Nino to family and friends, is a Roman Catholic and a father of nine. Born in New Jersey in 1936, he was educated at Georgetown University and Harvard Law School, then became a law professor at the University of Virginia and a lawyer under Presidents Richard Nixon and Gerald Ford. He was appointed to the Supreme Court in 1986 by President Ronald Reagan and is the longest-serving justice on the current Court.

Scalia is a sharp thinker with a blunt, outspoken style. He is known for asking more questions during oral arguments than any other justice and for being very sure of himself in his written opinions. A strong conservative, Scalia argues that the death penalty is constitutional but abortion is not. Despite their very different views, Scalia and Kagan respect and like each other.

Justice Antonin Scalia, whom Kagan has befriended, has served on the Supreme Court since 1986.

that I will bear true faith and allegiance to the same; that I take this obligation freely, without any mental reservation or purpose of evasion; and that I will well and faithfully discharge the duties of the office on which I am about to enter. So help me God."[55] Then, in a public chamber before friends and reporters, Kagan took a second, judicial oath: "I do solemnly swear that I will administer justice without respect to persons, and do equal right to the poor and to the rich, and that I will faithfully and impartially discharge and perform all the duties incumbent upon me as associate justice of the Supreme Court under the Constitution and laws of the United States. So help me God."[56]

With that, Kagan became the 112th justice and the fourth woman to serve on the U.S. Supreme Court. For the first time in Court history, three of the nine justices—Ruth Bader Ginsburg, Sotomayor, and Kagan—are women. Two of the female justices also hold another distinction: Kagan is the youngest justice on the current Court, twenty-seven years younger than the oldest justice, Ginsburg.

Kagan had won the greatest honor of her life. She took some time to celebrate at a White House reception in her honor hosted by the president. Away from the cameras, she went out for steak dinners with family and friends. But there was not much time to relax.

Scrutiny of the newest Supreme Court justice had just begun.

Chapter 5

Personal Life in a New Spotlight

Although Elena Kagan had held high public office before reaching the high court, she had always been able to maintain her privacy in her personal life. That is much harder to do as a Supreme Court justice. Family, friends, colleagues, and Supreme Court of the United States (SCOTUS) watchers have helped ease her transition into her new role.

Proud and Protective: The Kagan Family

Kagan still has strong family ties in New York City. Until her death in 2008, Gloria Kagan still lived in the West End Avenue co-op where Elena grew up. The Upper West Side of today, however, is nothing like the gritty, multiethnic place of Kagan's childhood. Today it is one of New York's most exclusive neighborhoods. The average household income is twice the national average, and 75 percent of its residents are white. After their mother's death, the Kagan siblings sold the family's co-op for $1.325 million, a bargain for the area.

Elena's younger brother, Irving, still teaches American history and constitutional law at Hunter College High School. There he is known for faculty debates over politics and for his fiery classroom style. One of his fifteen-year-old students says, "A lot of teachers just sit down explaining things from a chair. But he walks around

Elena Kagan, Celebrity

Elena Kagan's natural warmth and style has won her fans beyond the world of Supreme Court bloggers and other SCOTUS watchers. Funny measures of her new celebrity are not normally associated with dignified Supreme Court justices. Kagan has nicknames in the press: Lady Kaga and the Divine Miss K. Back at Harvard, local student hangout Mr. Bartley's Gourmet Burgers has added a new item to the menu: "The Elena Kagan: A burger smothered with a liberal amount of salsa and grilled pineapple served with onion rings. $9.99."[1] In Washington, bloggers post excited reports of Kagan sightings.

The bemused justice says once the new-guy-on-the-Court publicity dies down, she expects people will lose interest in her quite ordinary life. Until then, she cannot help grinning when someone sees her on the street and shouts, "You go, girl!"[2]

1. Quoted in Agnes K. Sibilski. "Elena Kagan Gets Her Own Bartley's Burger." *Harvard Crimson*, May 17, 2010. www.thecrimson.com/article/2010/5/17/burger-elena-kagan-famous.
2. Elena Kagan. C-SPAN interview by Susan Swain. C-SPAN Supreme Court Project, December 9, 2010. www.c-spanvideo.org/program/297143-1.

the classroom and is huffing and puffing because he's so excited."[57] Kagan's older brother, Marc, now married with two children, is the fourth teacher in the Kagan family. He taught first at A. Philip Randolph Campus High School in Harlem. Today he teaches world history at the Bronx High School of Science, like Hunter one of the city's most highly ranked public schools. He seems to be just as spirited as the rest of the family. Says a sixteen-year-old student, "He yells. He definitely yells. He's a fan of that."[58]

Kagan's brothers (and her twenty-two-year old niece, an aide to a New York state senator) supported Kagan throughout the stressful confirmation process, sitting behind her at her Senate hearings and standing beside her at her swearing-in. They did their best, however, to stay out of the media blitz. Partly on the advice of the White House, they avoided interviews. But sometimes they could not contain their pride and admiration. Irving Kagan told NPR reporter Ailsa Chang he wanted people to know how happy he was for his sister. Like Elena, he only wished their parents were alive to see her join the Supreme Court: "My parents would be over the top about this, just thrilled. . . . This would be the fulfillment of everything they would have hoped for."[59]

Kagan's brother Irving, right, was among several family members who attended her Senate confirmation hearings in June 2010.

New Digs

Before Kagan joined the Court, only Justice Ruth Bader Ginsburg actually lived inside the city limits of Washington, D.C. John Roberts commutes from his home in Maryland. Antonin Scalia, Clarence Thomas, Anthony Kennedy, and Samuel Alito live in Virginia. When the Court is not in session, Sonia Sotomayor returns to her Greenwich Village home in New York City, and Stephen Breyer goes home to Marlborough, Massachusetts.

Kagan moved to Washington when she became solicitor general in 2009. She sold the Cambridge condo where she lived during her years at Harvard for $1.5 million and moved into a luxury D.C. apartment building. Always a city girl, she seems to have decided to make her permanent home in the District of Columbia. In January 2011 Kagan was spotted inspecting houses for sale in the historic Logan Circle neighborhood, only about 1 mile (1.6km) from the Supreme Court building.

She could afford to live wherever she wants. By managing her finances remarkably well and living within her means, Kagan has become a millionaire. According to the financial statements she must file as a high government official, she saves money and does not make risky investments. Most impressively, she has zero debt of any kind.

Kagan's Personal Style

In looks and manner, Kagan is attractive but unassuming. At fifty-one, she is a plump woman with short brown hair, warm brown eyes, and a big, dimpled smile. During her confirmation, descriptions of Kagan seemed to focus on one thing—her height. The reports were relentless: Boy, is Elena Kagan short. *Daily Show* host Jon Stewart mocked the mainstream media for finding nothing better to talk about than this nonissue: "For [goodness] sake, she's 5'3"! That's not unreasonable! It's not like you would see her and go 'Oh my god, what happened to *her?*' This is *boring!*"[60]

Kagan endured especially harsh and undeserved public attacks on her looks from anti–Barack Obama, anti-Kagan camps. Right-wing radio talk show hosts and Internet bloggers hooted

Kagan came under far more scrutiny (and unfair criticism) for her personal appearance than male Supreme Court nominees are subjected to.

that she looked like a football linebacker, the cartoon ogre Shrek, and worse.

In the media buzz stirred up by these insults, many thoughtful people came to Kagan's defense. One contributor to the online news site *Daily Beast* wrote, "Why [does Kagan] have to put up with these comments? . . . Attractiveness is not exactly a qualification for judicial office. Not all the male justices on the Supreme Court are eye candy, but their confirmations didn't trigger this kind of ridicule."[61]

Writer and rabbi Naomi Levy spoke for many when she urged Kagan critics to get their priorities straight: "When evaluating a Supreme Court justice, substance matters, character matters, intellect matters, a nominee's judgment matters—but looks? . . . Who should be making the decisions that will affect our nation's future? Someone with the right measurements or someone with the right legal knowledge?"[62]

Kagan's wardrobe reflects her modest manner. In court, she sometimes tucks a plain white scarf into the neckline of her black judge's robe. She does not wear the lacy cravat—or "neck doily"—worn by Ginsburg and Sotomayor. As Kagan told one interviewer, "I think you just have to do what makes you feel comfortable. In my real life I'm not a kind of frilly, lacy person."[63] Besides, Kagan says, adding too many personal touches goes against the meaning of putting on the black robe. While that robe is on, the wearer disappears in a way; personal views are not supposed to show when the law is applied.

In official settings outside the courtroom, she wears tasteful, tailored suits with a pearl necklace and earrings. In her private life, she is a normal person who likes comfortable clothes and is not embarrassed to be seen in sneakers and "mom jeans."[64]

Of course, Kagan dresses up for the occasion, but even at her most formal she does not take herself too seriously. In September 2010, for instance, she attended the Washington Opera's season-opening gala at the Kennedy Center with the recently widowed Justice Ginsburg. The press showed up at the glittering affair to photograph Washington high society and their designer fashions. When Kagan, in a striking black cocktail dress and diamond earrings, was asked, "Who are you wearing tonight?" she grinned and replied, "I don't know. I just got this today!"[65]

Daily Life in the District

Outside of work, Kagan likes opera, friendly poker games, and rereading Jane Austen's *Pride and Prejudice.* She is said to prefer eating out with friends to cooking at home. She is also said to have favorite take-out in her adopted hometown: Indian food from Merzi, pizza from We the Pizza, and Popeyes chicken.

As might be expected from a proud teacher who has spent a lifetime interpreting and applying the law, Kagan now identifies herself with Conservative Judaism. This branch of the faith gives rabbis more leeway to interpret and apply Jewish law than the stricter Orthodox Judaism of her childhood.

Justice Kagan expects no special treatment in her private life. She proved this in January 2011 when she showed up for jury duty like any other citizen. Kagan was spotted sitting patiently in a crowd of prospective jurors in a waiting lounge at D.C. Superior Court. Casually dressed, she read and marked papers as she waited.

Trial lawyers must have been relieved when one of the most brilliant legal scholars in the country was not called to the jury selection room. When Kagan and the rest of the jury pool were released, she chatted graciously with a few people who recognized her. Then, her civic duty done, she dropped her plastic badge in a trash bin and quietly left without picking up her four-dollar transportation allowance.

Staying Active Under New Rules

Kagan is on record as donating $7,450 to various Democratic candidates, $4,600 of that total to Obama, from 2000 to 2008. Technically, as a Supreme Court justice she *could* continue to make campaign donations and speeches supporting one party or another. Unlike other judges, Supreme Court justices have no official code of ethics that bans shows of political favoritism.

In practice, however, Kagan and her fellow justices avoid activities that make them look biased. Kagan is still allowed to vote, like any other adult citizen. It would look bad, however, for her to participate in political fund-raising activities—including attending or making speeches at fund-raising dinners or accepting payment for travel expenses from outside political groups.

Kagan has found other, acceptable outlets for activism, such as participating in forums on women's rights issues. For example, on October 26, 2010, Kagan attended the annual Women's Conference in Long Beach, California. This event draws well-known women in politics, business, media, and the arts, such as its founder, Maria Shriver, and ABC News anchor Diane Sawyer. In 2010 brand-new justice Kagan went to the meeting with all three of the women who have served on the Court before her: Justices Ginsburg and Sotomayor and retired justice Sandra Day O'Connor.

Diane Sawyer moderates a panel discussion with the four female Supreme Court justices at the 2010 Women's Conference in Long Beach, California. Kagan has continued her advocacy for women's rights issues while serving on the Court.

At the conference, the three veteran justices—affectionately dubbed "the Supremes"—talked about their pride in Kagan's appointment and their own struggles to be accepted as equals on the Supreme Court. O'Connor, the first female justice in U.S. history, described visiting the Court at the beginning of Kagan's first term: "I looked up at the bench on which I sat for 25 years and what did I see? On the far right, a woman. On the left side, a woman. And in the middle, a woman. And it was dazzling."[66]

Ginsburg said wryly, "For the first time, the public can see that we are really there to stay. In the years I served with Sandra, every year without fail, one lawyer or another called me 'Justice

"The Supremes"

The three women who preceded Elena Kagan on the high court have very different backgrounds. Texas-born Sandra Day O'Connor grew up on a cattle ranch in Arizona. A white Protestant Republican and the mother of three sons, she was elected to the Arizona Senate before becoming a judge. Ronald Reagan appointed her to the Supreme Court in 1981. After she stepped down in 2006, O'Connor became the chancellor of the College of William and Mary in Virginia.

Ruth Bader Ginsburg is a white Jewish Democrat, born and raised in Brooklyn, New York, and the mother of two. A lifelong women's rights activist and liberal, Ginsburg was a professor of law and federal judge before Bill Clinton appointed her to the Court in 1993.

Sonia Sotomayor, the Court's first Hispanic justice, was born and raised in the Bronx and identifies herself as Nuyorican, a slang term for Puerto Rican Americans from New York. A Roman Catholic liberal Democrat, Sotomayor has no children. She was a longtime federal appeals court judge before being appointed to the Court in 2009 by Barack Obama.

The four women to serve on the Supreme Court, from left, retired Justice O'Connor, Justice Sotomayor, Justice Ginsburg, and Justice Kagan, pose together following Kagan's investiture ceremony in October 2010.

O'Connor.' And we really don't look alike. . . . This year, I am confident no one will call Justice Kagan 'Justice Ginsburg' or 'Justice Sotomayor.'"[67]

Still Inspiring Students

In May 2011 Kagan went back to campus, this time as the key speaker at the University of New Mexico School of Law graduation ceremony in Albuquerque. It was her first public speech since her SCOTUS swearing-in nine months earlier. Given the many steps in Kagan's career, it took a while for the school's dean to introduce his honored guest. She took the microphone and joked, "The secret is I can't keep a job, but I think I've solved that problem now."[68]

With nostalgia, she relived her own days as a law student and law professor. Just as she had been taught the value of public service in high school, she urged the graduating class to "find a way to give back."[69]And with typical warmth, she personally gave each graduate a hug and a handshake.

"Do What You Love"

Elena Kagan's first public speech as a Supreme Court justice was to the graduating class of the University of New Mexico School of Law in May 2011. Her advice to the graduates spells out the principles she lives by: "You should now and always do what you love. You should immerse yourself in the problems you think most important and challenging, surround yourself with people you think most interesting, throw yourself into whatever has the greatest prospect of giving meaning to your life and providing satisfaction and excitement. Do what you love."

Quoted in Susan Montoya Bryan. "Kagan Shares Wisdom with UNM Law Graduates." *Santa Fe New Mexican*, May 14, 2011.

Kagan delivers the commencement address at the University of New Mexico School of Law in May 2011, urging graduates to consider public service.

"You're Part of the Institution"

Kagan had gotten a special initiation of her own on the day she was sworn in as Supreme Court justice. She was met by Chief Justice Roberts, who took her on a brief tour of the building's inner rooms, starting with the robing room. There against the wall was a row of wood lockers with brass nameplates. Kagan passed the names: first the chief justice, followed by Justice Stevens, and so on down to the last locker, Justice Sotomayor's.

Roberts showed Kagan around the building for only about fifteen minutes. As Kagan tells it: "We ended up back at the robing room again. And in that fifteen-minute time . . . Justice Stevens's name had come off and each of the nameplates had

Kagan, left, walks with Chief Justice John Roberts in front of the Supreme Court following her investiture ceremony in October 2010.

gone over one, and now there was a Justice Kagan. . . . It was a very effective way to say to me, 'Well, you're here now. You're part of the community. You're part of the institution.' It was a very powerful thing to see."[70]

As she has done in Chicago and Cambridge, Kagan is making the most of what her adopted city of Washington, D.C., has to offer. She has been warmly welcomed by her colleagues and by D.C. friends and neighbors. She would be under a great deal more scrutiny professionally during her first term on the Supreme Court.

Chapter 6

Getting Down to Work

Getting down to work on the Supreme Court of the United States means following more than 220 years of tradition. The Court's term—the time of year when it is officially in session—always begins on the first Monday in October and ends the following June. Its calendar is a mix of three kinds of workdays. On oral argument days (open to the public) lawyers on both sides of a case stand before the justices and take their questions. On conference days the justices gather behind closed doors to discuss and debate cases. The rest of the days are nonargument days, when the justices read, write, and study cases separately in their offices.

Elena Kagan's first term began on October 4, 2010, an oral argument day. On that Monday, as always, the justices gathered in the robing room to put on the identical black robes that symbolize impartial justice. As always, before the justices entered the courtroom they all shook hands.

The chief justice entered the courtroom first. The eight associate justices filed in behind him, with Kagan in last place. All nine took their seats in a traditional order. Chief Justice John Roberts sits in the center black-leather chair. According to seniority, Antonin Scalia sits to Roberts's right, Anthony Kennedy to Roberts's left. The rest alternate sides by seniority, with the two newest justices on the ends. From the viewpoint of a visitor facing the long bench, Sonia Sotomayor moved to the far left when Kagan joined the Court, and Kagan now sits at the far right.

These traditions are meant to remind the justices that they are part of a process that is greater than themselves. What is important is the institution of the Supreme Court and the unbiased application of the law, not the individuals of the Supreme Court and their personal views.

The New Justice's Duties

Kagan has several duties in her position as junior associate justice. First, she is assigned to review a chunk of the cases that are appealed each year to the Supreme Court. Her chunk comes from the Sixth and Seventh Circuits, two of the thirteen geographical divisions at the second-highest level in the U.S. court system. Kagan has the power to grant stays in these cases, meaning she can put a hold on the lower-court verdict so it cannot take effect until the Supreme Court rules on the case.

Justice Kagan, second from right, joins the other justices for her first session as a member of the Supreme Court in October 2010. From left are Justice Clarence Thomas, Justice Sonia Sotomayor, Justice Antonin Scalia, Justice Stephen Breyer, Chief Justice John Roberts, Justice Samuel Alito, Justice Anthony Kennedy, Kagan, and Justice Ruth Bader Ginsburg.

Kagan's best-known duty is the public face of the Court. She hears both sides of a case, questions and debates the lawyers who are arguing the case, and discusses the case with her fellow justices. Then she votes to affirm or reverse the lower-court verdict. (On extremely rare and urgent occasions, a case goes directly to the Supreme Court without first being heard at lower levels.) Sometimes she is assigned to write the official majority opinion. If she strongly disagrees with the majority vote, she can also write a dissenting opinion, permanently attached to the majority opinion, that explains why she thinks the vote should have gone the other way.

As the most junior associate justice, Kagan also has to take notes and pass messages to the Court clerks when the justices are meeting in the conference room (no one but the justices may enter this room). In another Court tradition, she also has to answer knocks at the conference room door and hold the door when her fellow justices enter and leave.

Members of the Supreme Court take their traditional front-row seat at President Barack Obama's State of the Union Address in January 2011. From left are Chief Justice Roberts, Justice Kennedy, Justice Ginsburg, Justice Breyer, Justice Sotomayor, and Justice Kagan.

Kagan says she is grateful for another conference-room custom: When a case is brought up, the chief justice gets to talk first, followed by the most senior associate, and so on. No one is allowed to interrupt or question another justice until everyone at the table has had one turn. As the last in line, Kagan says it is nice to know she will get a chance to speak before free-for-all arguments start.

Most of the justices also feel a duty to attend the president's annual State of the Union Address in the Capitol. This can be an unpleasant duty. The Supreme Court is supposed to be above politics, and some justices have said they would prefer not to be part of what they see as a partisan pep rally. Moreover, presidents have criticized Supreme Court decisions in their speech, and the justices do not like sitting through such a scolding publicly, and on camera.

The Perks of a Supreme Court Justice

All associate justices earn the same annual salary, no matter how long they have served. In Kagan's first term, that was $213,900. (The chief justice earned $223,500.) Continuing a 150-year tradition, Kagan will draw her full pay for the rest of her life, even after she quits or retires. With summers off, she will have free time to write books or give speeches for additional income, if she chooses.

Besides the obvious benefits of lifetime job security and the prestige of the position, the job of Supreme Court justice has other enviable perks. Perhaps most important, the justices have some control over their own workload. Together they decide which cases they will add to the docket, or calendar, for the upcoming term. (Sometimes they do not actually get to a docketed case, or they start a case but need more time to decide it. These cases are postponed, or carried forward to the next term.) Out of the thousands of petitions the Court receives each year, the justices may hear as few as seventy appeals. The average is around one hundred.

Kagan is entitled to have up to four law clerks to help her with her own workload. Some members of the current Court reportedly delegate most of their opinion writing to their clerks, who are chosen from among the brightest young law school graduates in the country, just as Marshall chose Kagan in 1986. The clerks on Kagan's team for the 2010–2011 term were Andrew Crespo, Elizabeth B. Prelogar, and Trisha Anderson, all Harvard Law graduates; and Yale Law School graduate Allon Kedem, who was already clerking for Kennedy when Kagan tapped him for the job.

Kagan also gets an office with a fireplace and artwork borrowed from the Smithsonian museums. If she feels like getting some exercise, she can use the top-floor basketball court. (No playing allowed during oral arguments, though: The noise of bouncing basketballs and pounding feet comes right down into the courtroom.)

Kagan Recusals

Impressive benefits and perks notwithstanding, Supreme Court justices have a very heavy workload. Kagan's first-term load was lighter than her colleagues', however, because of recusals.

Recusal means the disqualification of a judge from hearing arguments and ruling on a case because the judge could be prejudiced in favor of one side or the other or could somehow gain from a decision one way or the other. A Supreme Court justice can recuse himself or herself or be recused on the objection of the other justices. Recusal is not a trivial matter. The consequence is that only eight justices vote on a case, which on today's divided Court likely means a number of 4–4 tie votes. In the event of a tie, the lower court verdict stands; that is, the Supreme Court cannot overturn the lower court's decision.

Kagan recused herself from twenty-five cases on the Court's 2010–2011 calendar because she dealt with them in some way as solicitor general. No matter how little she had to do with these cases, she was working for the president at the time. This means she could be accused of bias or conflict of interest that would make her vote as a justice less than fair. In practice, recusal means more than not being able to vote on a case. As a recused justice, Kagan had to get up and leave the courtroom or conference room whenever the case was being discussed or argued.

During the 2010–2011 term, the Court decided nineteen cases without Kagan. Only one of these, however, resulted in a tie vote. That was a copyright battle between Costco and the Swiss watchmaker Omega. The Swiss company wanted Costco to stop buying luxury Omega brand watches overseas where they are cheap, importing them to America, and selling them below retail price in Costco stores. Omega had won the case in the lower court. The tie vote meant the lower-court verdict stands.

Omega watches are displayed for sale at a Costco store. During the 2010–2011 term, the Court decided nineteen cases from which Kagan was recused, including one in which the Swiss watchmaker Omega sued warehouse retailer Costco over its practices for importing and selling its watches.

The 2010–2011 Docket with Kagan

Today's Supreme Court is what is known as a hot bench. During oral arguments, the justices ask lots of questions and test lawyers on their reasoning. The justices talk to each other, too; sometimes the lawyer at the podium just stands there while the justices argue among themselves. From the first day of the term, Kagan was ready and willing to jump in, on the bench and in writing.

In one case she called the campaign activities of a Louisiana man running for local office "an assortment of dirty tricks."[71] In another, just before she launched into a complicated decision full of legal jargon, she told the full courtroom, "If you understand anything I say here, you'll likely be a lawyer, and you will have had your morning cup of coffee."[72]

Kagan's most blistering language came in an Arizona campaign finance case she first heard in March 2011. During oral arguments Kagan came down firmly on the side of a voter-approved law that gave extra public campaign funds to candidates who faced being outspent by privately funded rivals. From the bench, she said, "I think the purpose of this law is to prevent corruption. That's . . . the purpose of all public financing systems."[73]

The Court's conservative majority voted 5–4 to strike down the Arizona law. Kagan responded by writing a thirty-two-page dissenting opinion. In what legal analyst Jess Bravin called "a full-blast dissent, using pointed . . . sometimes sarcastic language rarely seen from the Court's liberal minority,"[74] Kagan coolly wrote that any ordinary citizen without a law degree could see this decision violated the First Amendment.

Kagan also wrote a powerful dissent in another Arizona case, involving the separation of church and state. It is unconstitutional for the government to use taxpayer money to pay, for example, for children to attend private religious schools. The Court ruled 5–4, however, that taxpayers cannot object if a state allows people to subtract from the taxes they owe the government money they give to groups called school tuition organiza-

The SCOTUS Split

Supreme Court justices are often compared to umpires: They do not make the rules; they just apply them. Like umpires, however, justices can look at the same issue and call it differently. Today's Court is split down the middle, with a group of conservative justices who very often agree on one side and a group of liberal (or progressive) justices who very often agree on the other.

The four Supreme Court of the United States (SCOTUS) conservatives are Antonin Scalia, Clarence Thomas, John G. Roberts Jr., and Samuel Alito. All are Republican appointees. The four SCOTUS liberals are Ruth Bader Ginsburg, Stephen Breyer, Sonia Sotomayor, and Elena Kagan. All are Democratic appointees.

In close decisions, ninth justice Anthony Kennedy has been cast as the all-important swing vote that both wings of the Court try to win over. Appointed by Republican president Ronald Reagan in 1988, Kennedy usually votes with the conservatives. (In the 2010–2011 term, sixteen cases were decided by 5–4 votes. Ten of those cases were split four conservatives against four liberals, with Kennedy supplying the fifth vote for the conservative side.) However, he is a little more likely than other justices on the right to be a moderate—someone who has a conservative point of view on some issues and a liberal point of view on others.

tions, which use that money to pay for children to attend private religious schools. In her dissenting opinion, Kagan argued that these dollars, whether they are called a tax credit or a cash payment, are government dollars being used to pay for religious activity.

Not all of Kagan's first-term rulings were dramatic or controversial. For example, her first written majority opinion as a Supreme Court justice, delivered on January 11, 2011, sided with a credit card company in a bankruptcy dispute. Without fanfare, the Court ruled 8–1 against the debtor.

A Dazzling Range of Issues

Plenty of SCOTUS decisions did make headlines. For example, the case of *Snyder v. Phelps* involved the Westboro Baptist Church's right to picket the funeral of a Marine killed in Iraq, carrying signs with hateful messages that hurt and angered the dead soldier's family. Kagan voted with the majority, 8–1, that no matter how offensive the signs were, they are protected by the First Amendment right to free speech.

Connick v. Thompson pitted a Louisiana man who served eighteen years on death row against a New Orleans district attorney who failed to give the court evidence that the man was innocent. A lower court had awarded the released inmate $14 million in

A member of the Westboro Baptist Church protests in front of the Supreme Court in October 2010. Kagan voted with the Court's 8–1 majority ruling in Snyder v. Phelps *that the church's demonstrations at soldiers' funerals, although offensive, were protected under the First Amendment.*

The Next Empty Seat

As Elena Kagan settles into her new role, Supreme Court of the United States (SCOTUS) watchers have turned to a new question: Will there soon be another empty seat to fill on the Supreme Court? As Democrats and Republicans think of scenarios that could give them an edge on the Court, they usually focus on Justice Ruth Bader Ginsburg. There are three reasons for the sense of urgency attached to the question: First, Ginsburg is in her late seventies, the oldest justice, and her health is uncertain. Second, the current Court has a narrow 5–4 conservative majority. Third, President Barack Obama is up for reelection in 2012.

If the liberal Ginsburg were to retire, Democrats hope she would choose to do so while Obama is in office, as he is more likely to name a replacement whose views are aligned with Ginsburg's. If Obama loses the election to a Republican candidate, and *then* Ginsburg steps down, her replacement would likely be a conservative. The balance of the Court would shift further to the right.

In July 2011 Ginsburg tried to put some of this speculation to rest. According to reporter Mark Sherman, "Ginsburg has said gracefully, and with apparent good humor, that the president should not expect a retirement letter before 2015."

Mark Sherman. "Ruth Bader Ginsburg Talks Supreme Court Retirement Plans." *Huffpost Politics*, July 2, 2011. www.huffingtonpost.com/2011/07/02/ruth-bader-ginsburg-supreme-court-retirement_n_889260.html.

damages. But SCOTUS voted 5–4 that the district attorney was not responsible for a staff mistake and did not have to pay the $14 million. Kagan was one of the four justices who disagreed with this ruling.

The 2010–2011 docket gave the justices a fascinating variety of issues to resolve. Kagan and her colleagues ruled, for example, that the state of California must reduce its prison population by thirty-three thousand inmates to reduce overcrowding. They also lifted the ban on selling violent video games such as *Mortal Kombat* to minors.

The Post-Game Wrap-Up

The busy 2010–2011 SCOTUS term ended June 27, 2010. The Court had rendered eighty-five opinions. Sixteen of these were 5–4 decisions. Roberts and Alito agreed on almost every vote, just as Kagan and Sotomayor did. On the other hand, almost half of the Court's decisions were unanimous, proving that the SCOTUS "umpires" often do see plays the same way.

In a C-SPAN interview, Kagan confessed that she sometimes felt overwhelmed during her first term. "It's sort of drinking out of a fire hose, you know. It's always something new, something different," she said. "The learning curve is extremely steep . . . sometimes it seems vertical."[75] SCOTUS watchers and law professors, however, gave her high marks. Law professor John McGinnis was most impressed: "She has gotten off to as strong a start as John Roberts did when he became chief justice. . . . She, Roberts, and Scalia clearly are the best writers on the court."[76]

The Robe Suits Her Well

Midway through Kagan's first term, NPR legal affairs correspondent Nina Totenberg reported that the justice was already blooming in her new role. "Elena Kagan is where she's always wanted to be, and she loves being there," Totenberg said. "As a friend told her after seeing the new justice just two months after she was sworn in, 'Man, does life tenure suit you well.'"[77]

Kagan does seem to be fitting in on the high court. Always eager to build new bridges, she asked Scalia to take her skeet shooting, one of Scalia's favorite hobbies. He happily obliged. She told classmates at a Harvard Law School reunion that she is now known as the frozen yogurt justice because she helped get a frozen yogurt machine installed in the Supreme Court lunchroom. Following O'Connor's custom, she encourages the justices to eat lunch together. Just as she once handed out free coffee to get bickering professors to sit down and talk to each other, she looks for small gestures to strengthen working relationships with her new colleagues.

Kagan arrived at the Supreme Court aiming to bridge partisan differences. If she fails to shift the Court closer to the center,

Kagan poses wearing her judicial robe. In her short time on the Court, she has worked to establish ties with her fellow justices and bridge partisan differences.

she will not be the first judge who arrived with the same goal and left disappointed. Whatever her ultimate role, she brings valuable assets to the Supreme Court: intelligence, integrity, and the passion for the law that has made her so successful in classrooms and public service for twenty-five years. Kagan explains the core belief that keeps her going: "Through most of my professional life, I've had the simple joy of teaching. Of trying to communicate to students why I so love the law, not just because it's challenging and endlessly interesting . . . but *because law matters*. Because it keeps us safe. Because it protects our most fundamental rights and freedoms, and because it is the foundation of our democracy."[78]

Notes

Introduction: Elena Kagan: Bridge Builder on a Divided Supreme Court

1. Quoted in Jeffrey Rosen. "At Center Court: Can Kagan Be a Consensus Builder?" *Time*, May 13, 2010. www.time.com/time/magazine/article/0,9171,1989126,00.html.
2. Quoted in Ariane de Vogue. "Elena Kagan: Life of 'Learning and Study of the Law,'" ABC News.com, May 10, 2010. http://abcnews.go.com/Politics/elena-kagan-solicitor-general-intellectual-heft-knowledge-law/story?id=10602944.
3. Larry D. Kramer et al. Joint letter to the chairmen of the Senate Judiciary Committee, June 7, 2010. http://judiciary.senate.gov/nominations/SupremeCourt/upload/060710JointLetter.pdf.
4. Elena Kagan. "Elena Kagan, in Her Own Words." Video. White House, May 11, 2010. www.whitehouse.gov/photos-and-video/video/elena-kagan-her-own-words.

Chapter 1: Coming of Age in a Politically Turbulent Era

5. Quoted in Peter S. Green and Kristin Jensen. "Kagan's Diverse, 'Decrepit' Manhattan Helped Shape Her Outlook." *Bloomberg*, June 25, 2010. www.bloomberg.com/news/2010-06-25/nominee-kagan-s-diverse-decrepit-manhattan-helped-shape-her-development.html.
6. Quoted in Lisa W. Foderaro and Christine Haughney. "The Kagan Family: Left-Leaning and Outspoken." *New York Times*, June 18, 2010.
7. Quoted in Jesse Lee. "Nominating Kagan: 'Her Passion for the Law Is Anything But Academic.'" *White House Blog*, May 10, 2010. www.whitehouse.gov/blog/2010/05/10/nominating-kagan-her-passion-law-anything-academic.
8. Blake Eskin. "The Ghost of Mrs. Kagan." *News Desk* (blog), *New Yorker*, May 10, 2010. www.newyorker.com/online/blogs/newsdesk/2010/05/the-ghost-of-mrs-kagan.html.

9. Quoted in Eskin. "The Ghost of Mrs. Kagan."

10. Quoted in Foderaro and Haughney. "The Kagan Family."

11. Quoted in Sheryl Gay Stolberg, Katharine Q. Seelye, and Lisa W. Foderaro. "A Climb Marked by Confidence and Canniness." *New York Times*, May 10, 2010. www.nytimes.com/2010/05/10/us/politics/10kagan.html.

12. Quoted in Stolberg, Seelye, and Foderaro. "A Climb Marked by Confidence and Canniness."

13. Quoted in Stolberg, Seelye, and Foderaro. "A Climb Marked by Confidence and Canniness."

14. Elena Kagan. "November 10, 1980: Fear and Loathing in Brooklyn." *Daily Princetonian*, November 10, 1980. www.dailyprincetonian.com/2010/05/03/26082.

15. Elena Kagan. C-SPAN interview by Susan Swain. C-SPAN Supreme Court Project, December 9, 2010. www.c-spanvideo.org/program/297143-1.

16. Kagan. C-SPAN interview by Susan Swain.

Chapter 2: Climbing the Career Ladder

17. Quoted in Greg Hinz. "Ab Mikva Talks About His Ex-Clerk, Elena Kagan." *Greg Hinz on Politics* (blog), *Chicago Business*, May 10, 2010. www.chicagobusiness.com/section/blogs?blogID=greg-hinz&plckController=Blog&plckScript=blogscript&plckElementId=blogdest&plckBlogPage=BlogViewPost&plckPostId=Blog%3A1daca073-2eab-468e-9f19-ec177090a35cPost%3Acf97d174-0212-488a-9153-b09a1e0c9fe7&sid=sitelife.chicagobusiness.com.

18. Elena Kagan. Testimony before the Senate Judiciary Committee. "Panel I: Elena Kagan to Be Solicitor General of the United States Department of Justice." February 10, 2009. http://judiciary.senate.gov/hearings/hearing.cfm?id=e655f9e2809e5476862f735da14362b2.

19. Elena Kagan. "Confirmation Messes, Old and New." *University of Chicago Law Review*, Spring 1995, p. 941.

20. John Podesta. Transcript of White House media conference call. Federal News Service, May 19, 2010. www6.lexisnexis.com/publisher/EndUser?Action=UserDisplayFullDocument&orgId=574&topicId=25188&docId=l:1189829940&start=8.

21. Josh Gottheimer. Transcript of White House media conference call. Federal News Service, May 19, 2010. www6.lexis nexis.com/publisher/EndUser?Action=UserDisplayFullDoc ument&orgId=574&topicId=25188&docId=l:1189829940 &start=8.

22. Neera Tanden. Transcript of White House media conference call. Federal News Service, May 19, 2010. www6.lexisnexis .com/publisher/EndUser?Action=UserDisplayFullDocume nt&orgId=574&topicId=25188&docId=l:1189829940&s tart=8.

23. Kagan. "Confirmation Messes, Old and New," p. 936.

24. Kagan. "Confirmation Messes, Old and New," p. 934.

25. Kagan. "Confirmation Messes, Old and New," p. 939.

Chapter 3: From the White House to Academia and Back

26. Drake Bennett. "Crimson Tide." *Boston Globe*, October 19, 2008. www.boston.com/bostonglobe/ideas/articles/2008/10/19/crimson_tide.

27. Quoted in Bennett. "Crimson Tide."

28. Quoted in Bennett. "Crimson Tide."

29. Quoted in Megan Woolhouse. "She's Thawed Harvard Law." *Boston Globe*, January 4, 2009. www.boston.com/news/poli tics/2008/articles/2009/01/04/shes_thawed_harvard_law.

30. Quoted in Bennett. "Crimson Tide."

31. Quoted in Ameena Schelling. "Reserved Passion: Kagan '81." *Daily Princetonian*, May 3, 2010. www.dailyprinceto nian.com/2010/05/03/26081.

32. Quoted in Bennett. "Crimson Tide."

33. Kagan. "Elena Kagan, in Her Own Words."

34. Testimony of Elena Kagan. "Panel I: Elena Kagan to Be Solicitor General of the United States Department of Justice." Hearing before the Senate Judiciary Committee, February 10, 2009. http://judiciary.senate.gov/hearings/hearing.cfm?id=e655f9e2809e5476862f735da14362b2.

35. Kagan. "Panel I."

36. Kagan. "Panel I."

37. Kagan. "Panel I."
38. Quoted in Rosen. "At Center Court."

Chapter 4: Reaching the Pinnacle: The Supreme Court Confirmation Process

39. Glenn Greenwald. "The Case Against Elena Kagan." *Salon*, April 13, 2010. www.salon.com/news/opinion/glenn_green wald/2010/04/13/kagan.
40. Phyllis Schlafly. "Kagan Must Answer Question About DOMA." Eagle Forum, July 16, 2010. www.eagleforum.org/column/2010/july10/10-07-16.html.
41. Jeffrey T. Kuhner. "Obama the Destroyer." *Washington Times*, May 14, 2010. www.washingtontimes.com/news/2010/may/14/obama-the-destroyer.
42. Tom Goldstein. "9750 Words on Elena Kagan." *SCOTUS blog*, May 8, 2010. www.scotusblog.com/2010/05/9750-words-on-elena-kagan.
43. Quoted in Teddy Davis. "Justice Scalia Praises Elena Kagan's Lack of Judicial Experience." *Political Punch* (blog), ABC News, May 26, 2010. http://blogs.abcnews.com/political punch/2010/05/justice-scalia-praises-elena-kagans-lack-of-judicial-experience.html.
44. Quoted in Schelling. "Reserved Passion."
45. Quoted in *New York Times*. "Kagan's Notable Statements and Writings." May 9, 2010. www.nytimes.com/interac tive/2010/05/10/us/politics/20100505-kagan-opinions .html.
46. Quoted in *New York Times*. "Kagan's Notable Statements and Writings."
47. Opening statement of Elena Kagan. "The Nomination of Elena Kagan to Be an Associate Justice of the Supreme Court of the United States." Hearing before the Senate Judiciary Committee, June 28, 2010.
48. Quoted in opening statement of Elena Kagan. "The Nomination of Elena Kagan to Be an Associate Justice of the Supreme Court of the United States."
49. Opening statement of Elena Kagan. "The Nomination of Elena Kagan to Be an Associate Justice of the Supreme Court of the United States."

50. Elena Kagan. "Continuation of the Nomination of Elena Kagan to Be an Associate Justice of the Supreme Court of the United States." Hearing before the Senate Judiciary Committee, June 29, 2010.

51. Kagan. "Continuation of the Nomination of Elena Kagan to Be an Associate Justice of the Supreme Court of the United States." June 29, 2010.

52. Kagan. "Continuation of the Nomination of Elena Kagan to Be an Associate Justice of the Supreme Court of the United States." June 29, 2010.

53. Amy Klobuchar. "Continuation of the Nomination of Elena Kagan to Be an Associate Justice of the Supreme Court of the United States." Hearing before the Senate Judiciary Committee, June 30, 2010.

54. Elena Kagan. "Continuation of the Nomination of Elena Kagan to Be an Associate Justice of the Supreme Court of the United States." Hearing before the Senate Judiciary Committee, June 30, 2010.

55. 5 U.S.C., Section 3331.

56. 28 U.S.C., Section 453.

Chapter 5: Personal Life in a New Spotlight

57. Quoted in Foderaro and Haughney. "The Kagan Family."

58. Quoted in Foderaro and Haughney. "The Kagan Family."

59. Quoted in Ailsa Chang. "Kagan's Family in NYC: 'Just Incredibly Proud.'" WNYC, National Public Radio, June 28, 2010. www.wnyc.org/articles/wnyc-news/2010/jun/28/kagans-family-in-nyc-just-incredibly-proud.

60. Jon Stewart. The Daily Show. Comedy Central, May 11, 2010. www.thedailyshow.com/watch/tue-may-11-2010/release-the-kagan.

61. Deborah L. Rhode. "Why Elena Kagan's Looks Matter." Daily Beast, June 26, 2010. www.thedailybeast.com/articles/2010/06/26/elena-kagans-looks-and-why-they-matter.html.

62. Quoted in Mark Pearlman. "Elena Kagan, Eye Candy Mentality, and Jewish Wisdom." Jewish Week, July 7, 2010. www.thejewishweek.com/news/jinsider/elena_kagan_eye_candy_mentality_jewish_wisdom.

63. Kagan. C-SPAN interview by Susan Swain.
64. Quoted in David Lat. "The Eyes of the Law: Justices Eat Pizza Too." *Above the Law.* October 18, 2010. http://abovethelaw.com/2010/10/the-eyes-of-the-law-justices-eat-pizza-too/.
65. Quoted in Stephanie Green. "Elena Kagan, Ruth Bader Ginsburg Enjoy Glamorous Girls' Night." *Huffington Post*, September 13, 2010. www.huffingtonpost.com/stephanie-green/elena-kagan-last-minute-s_b_714788.html.
66. Quoted in Donna Schwartz Mills. "At the Women's Conference: 'The Supremes.'" *BlogHer* (blog), October 28, 2010. www.blogher.com/california-womens-conference-chat-supremes-sandra-day-oconnor-and-ruth-bader-ginsburg#_.
67. Quoted in Mills. "At the Women's Conference."
68. Quoted in Susan Montoya Bryan. "Kagan Shares Wisdom with UNM Law Graduates." *Santa Fe New Mexican*, May 14, 2011. www.santafenewmexican.com/local%20news/Kagan-shares-wisdom-with-UNM-law-graduates.
69. Quoted in Bryan. "Kagan Shares Wisdom with UNM Law Graduates."
70. Kagan. C-SPAN interview by Susan Swain.

Chapter 6: Getting Down to Work

71. Quoted in Jess Bravin. "Kagan Gives New Life to Court's Liberal Wing." *Wall Street Journal*, June 28, 2011. http://online.wsj.com/article/SB10001424052702303627104576414211191945474.html.
72. Quoted in Bill Mears. "Justice Kagan Stays Alert with a Little Bench Humor." CNN.com, June 16, 2011. http://articles.cnn.com/2011-06-16/us/scotus.kagan.humor_1_justice-elena-kagan-supreme-court-bayer-corp?_s=PM:US.
73. Quoted in Lee Ross. "Kagan Speaks Out on Public Financing of Elections." Fox News.com, March 28, 2011. www.foxnews.com/politics/2011/03/28/kagan-speaks-public-financing-elections/#.
74. Bravin. "Kagan Gives New Life to Court's Liberal Wing."
75. Kagan. C-SPAN interview by Susan Swain.
76. Quoted in Bravin. "Kagan Gives New Life to Court's Liberal Wing."

77. Nina Totenberg. "The Robe Seems to Suit New Justice Kagan." *Morning Edition*, NPR, December 27, 2010. www.npr.org/2010/12/27/132109642/the-robe-seems-to-suit-new-justice-kagan.
78. Quoted in Lee. "Nominating Kagan."

1960

Elena Kagan is born April 28 in New York City to Robert and Gloria Kagan. Brother Marc was born 1957; brother Irving is born 1965.

1973

Becomes bat mitzvah at Lincoln Square Synagogue.

1977

Graduates from Hunter College High School; enters Princeton University.

1980

Works for the unsuccessful campaign of Democrat Liz Holtzman to the U.S. Senate.

1981

Graduates summa cum laude from Princeton with a bachelor's degree in history; enters Oxford University.

1983

Earns a master's degree in philosophy from Oxford; enters Harvard Law School.

1986

Graduates with honors from Harvard Law; clerks for Judge Abner Mikva of the U.S. Court of Appeals for the D.C. Circuit.

1987

Clerks for Supreme Court justice Thurgood Marshall.

1989

Joins Washington, D.C., law firm Williams & Connolly.

1991

Becomes assistant professor of law at University of Chicago Law School.

1993

Takes leave of absence from Chicago Law to work for Senator Joe Biden during the Senate confirmation of Ruth Bader Ginsburg to the Supreme Court.

1994

Father, Robert Kagan, dies.

1995

Writes journal article "Confirmation Messes, Old and New" criticizing Supreme Court nominees for refusing to reveal their legal and personal views on controversial issues; becomes associate White House counsel under President Bill Clinton.

1997

Promoted to deputy assistant to the president for domestic policy and deputy director of the Domestic Policy Council.

1999

Joins Harvard Law School faculty as a visiting professor of law; two years later Kagan is granted tenure and becomes a full professor.

2003

Named first female dean of Harvard Law School; undertakes major reforms of school's curriculum, faculty, student life, and budget.

2008

Mother, Gloria Kagan, dies.

2009

Under President Barack Obama, becomes first female U.S. solicitor general; considered for Supreme Court seat vacated by retiring justice David Souter, but Obama nominates Sonia Sotomayor, who joins the Court in August.

2010

Justice John Paul Stevens announces retirement, April 10; Obama nominates Kagan to replace Stevens, May 10; Senate confirmation hearings, June 28–July 2; Kagan is sworn in as 112th justice and fourth woman on the Supreme Court, August 7; first term begins October 4.

2011

Delivers first written opinion January 11; first term ends June 27.

For More Information

Books

Jeffrey Toobin. *The Nine: Inside the Secret World of the Supreme Court.* New York: Anchor, 2008. A CNN legal analyst and longtime friend of Kagan focuses on the traits that have made SCOTUS justices great and not so great.

Scott Turow. *One L: The Turbulent True Story of a First Year at Harvard Law School.* New York, Penguin, 2010. An insider's look at the illustrious school where Kagan excelled in three roles: student, professor, and first female dean in Harvard Law history.

Periodicals

Joan Biskupic. "Justices Resume Routine Like They Don Robes." *USA Today.* October 5, 2010.

Joan Biskupic. "Supreme Court: 2010–11 Term in Review." *USA Today.* June 28, 2011.

Mary Kate Cary. "Elena Kagan's Effect on the Supreme Court." *U.S. News & World Report.* August 4, 2010.

Ronald Dworkin. "The Temptation of Elena Kagan." *New York Review of Books*, August 19, 2010.

Garrett Epps. "Justice Elena Kagan Speaks to America's Main Street." *Atlantic.* April 2011.

Dahlia Lithwick. "The Female Factor: Will Three Women Really Change the Court?" *Newsweek.* August 30, 2010.

Jay Newton-Small. "Supreme Court Hearings: Five Hot Topics for Elena Kagan." *Time,* June 28, 2010.

James Taranto. "The Kagan Principle." *Wall Street Journal.* July 1, 2011.

Internet Sources

Jess Bravin. "Kagan Gives New Life to Court's Liberal Wing." *Wall Street Journal*, June 28, 2011. http://online.wsj.com/article/SB10001424052702303627104576414211191945474.html?mod=googlenews_wsj.

Robert Farley and Angie Drobnic Holan. "Fact Checking the Claims on Elena Kagan." PolitiFact.com, May 10, 2010. www.politifact.com/truth-o-meter/article/2010/may/10/fact-check-elena-kagan.

Stanley Fish. "A Dollar Is a Dollar: Elena Kagan's Style." *New York Times*, April 11, 2011. http://opinionator.blogs.nytimes.com/2011/04/11/a-dollar-is-a-dollar-elena-kagans-style.

Glenn Greenwald. "The Case Against Elena Kagan." *Salon*, April 13, 2010. www.salon.com/news/opinion/glenn_greenwald/2010/04/13/kagan.

MediaMatters for America. "Myths and Falsehoods About Elena Kagan's Supreme Court Nomination." May 10, 2010. http://mediamatters.org/print/research/201005100001.

Remy Melina. "How Would Elena Kagan Change the Supreme Court?" *LiveScience*, May 11, 2010. www.livescience.com/8240-elena-kagan-change-supreme-court.html.

Stephanie Mencimer. "Why Do So Many People Think Elena Kagan Is Gay?" *Mother Jones*, May 11, 2010. http://motherjones.com/politics/2010/05/elena-kagan-gay-rumors-supreme-court#.

Donna Schwartz Mills. "At the Women's Conference: 'The Supremes.'" *BlogHer* (blog), October 28, 2010. www.blogher.com/california-womens-conference-chat-supremes-sandra-day-oconnor-and-ruth-bader-ginsburg#_.

Josh Nathan-Kazis. "Kagan's Hood: Liberal, Precocious, Very Jewish." *Forward*, May 12, 2010. www.forward.com/articles/127976.

Nina Totenberg. "The Robe Seems to Suit New Justice Kagan." *Morning Edition*, NPR, December 27, 2010. www.npr.org/2010/12/27/132109642/the-robe-seems-to-suit-new-justice-kagan.

Washington Post. "Supreme Court Round-Up, 2010-2011." June 28, 2011. www.washingtonpost.com/wp-srv/special/nation/scotus10-11/.

Websites

Kagan Confirmation Hearings, C-SPAN Video Library (www.c-spanvideo.org/program/KaganCo). An easy-to-view archive of Kagan's Senate confirmation hearings, June 28–July 2, 2010, offered in both full-length sessions and selected highlight clips. An excellent, first-person introduction to Kagan in her own words.

SCOTUSblog (www.scotusblog.com). This comprehensive, constantly updated blog offers Supreme Court news, case files, procedures, educational resources such as a glossary and biographies of the justices, and "In Plain English," a helpful, weekly column that explains Court decisions and their effects in clear, layman's terms.

Supreme Court (www.pbs.org/wnet/supremecourt). An educational site sponsored by PBS covering Supreme Court history, landmark cases, interviews of justices, the Constitution, and more through essays, ingenious interactive games, and classroom lesson plans.

Supreme Court Historical Society (www.supremecourthistory.org). Loads of information on the Court past and present, including history quizzes, links to an audio archive of oral arguments, journal articles, and a monthly newsletter.

Supreme Court of the United States (www.supremecourt.gov). The official site of the Supreme Court is the authority on recent decisions, the Court calendar and rules, and helpful information for visitors. The site offers transcripts of oral arguments and justices' speeches as well as overviews of Court procedures.

About the Author

Viqi Wagner is a textbook and legislative editor and a writer with a special interest in U.S. and international politics. She lives in Richmond, Virginia.